Kǒngmíng
A Memoir (of Sorts)

Brant von Goble

Loosey Goosey Press
Okemos, Michigan

Loosey Goosey Press
2222 W. Grand River Ave
Okemos, MI 48864

Copyright © 2025 Brant von Goble
(ISNI: 0000 0004 6433 5918)
License: CC Attribution-NonCommercial 4.0 International
(https://creativecommons.org/licenses/by-nc/4.0/)

ISBN: 979-8-9942789-0-1 (Hardcover)
ISBN: 979-8-9942789-1-8 (eBook)

Kǒngmíng

This is a story from a long time ago and very far away—a ghost story, a *guǐgùshi*. I hope, I *think* it's mostly true.

But who knows?

We die in each moment, and an imposter replaces us. The hauntings of our old selves trail behind, begging to be remembered, willing to say anything—to lie, if only by omission—to keep from being swallowed by the dark. They are not particular about times and dates, popping in as they please, bound by nothing more than impulse and desperation. So this is both my story and someone else's—someone dead, someone different by degree, or maybe forever living in the past, each moment crystal and frozen, eternal and instantaneous.

What I *do* know is this:

My first semester in Hunan was one of perfect unpreparedness. I was less than ready before I left the United States, but I'm never ready for anything before I start. And I had been un-preparing myself for a long time.

***

The email to my school account is ambiguous—*Want to teach in China? Come to our open house*—and what follows is a building and room number I have never seen before on a campus I have never visited. I reread the unadorned text, which does nothing to clarify matters. These are the aughts—the earlier days of online classes, before Zoom, before constant video chats and real-time messages. Odd missives from officials, teachers, and departments arrive without much rhyme, reason, or context. My master's program, through which I am slogging with minimal enthusiasm, is delivered asynchronously—download this, study that, and complete something else. The university, counties away, could be on a different continent for all the difference it would make.

Online classes are a deliberate choice for me. Driving around a campus for hours, fighting for parking, and all to hear someone drone on from books I could have as easily read by myself, knowing I would email or upload my papers regardless of how (or if) I met my teachers in meatspace. At best, this seems pointless; at worst, idiotic. At home, alone, is a better fit, and I have more time to edit my journal, *Gander Press Review*—a short story and poetry magazine that would hemorrhage money if it had any money to bleed.

I savor the distance online learning affords me—that I am *somewhere* and whatever I write and do—papers, assignments, bone-headed queries—is going *somewhere else*. There is comfort in knowing that *you* and *what you create* are separated by sufficient space, in knowing that not all the eggs of person and product are in the same basket of proximity.

The asynchrony of the master's program notwithstanding, it feels lightning fast compared to high school, done by way of paper correspondence, with return slips and late-night trips to a tiny rural post office with humming yellow lights and the sharp smell of gum stamps, and weeks of waiting to know a score. In graduate school, I am still drawn to the needle-tingle of distance, the call to move and send and go—somewhere, anywhere—as I imagine my coursework being converted, modulated, and transmitted through the wires and fibers.

***

My sole substantial connection to China is RTI—Radio Taiwan International—received not from distant Asia but from WYFR, a religious shortwave station that sold some of its broadcast time to the highest bidder. In this case, the

Taiwanese. So I was hearing China by way of Florida, from *O-kee-cho-bee*, as the fulsome Chinese voice announced at the top of the hour, making swampland sound fascinating, exotic.

That was a decade before I began my master's, when I was in the aforementioned correspondence high school, on the farm, my ear pressed close to the three-inch speaker of my Sangean shortwave on crisp winter nights, pulling words no one else could hear from the static. Still, the QSL cards, the bookmarks, the newspaper printed on onionskin paper, and the little contest prizes I received by way of airmail were enough to make a lasting impression on me, as were the signal reports and half-page achingly earnest essays I sent to Taipei. (Or maybe not—these are memories of memories of things I lost years ago—recollections of place far away and long ago about a time back further still.)

In retrospect, my interests in radio and its Cold War-era methods of communication and persuasion were archaic before I developed them. By the late 1990s, half the neighbors had mini-dishes and Xboxes. My listening sessions—extending often into the morning hours—my ham license, and the clanky/rattling Smith Corona I used to type my letters and lessons were decades behind the times. But my throwback life suited me better than not. We obliterate distance in the digital era—a tragic triumph of speed and convenience, a drive down the Interstate, the country reduced to indistinguishable round-pylon concrete bridges and well-marked exits—but I could still hear it then, in the whistling of space and crackling of stormy weather.

* * *

I miss the meeting. My love of going places aside, I have no sense of direction. GPS confuses me to no end, verbal instructions are worse, and I could no more identify a landmark than I could build one with both hands on a steering wheel. Every journey is stochastic, yielding considerable surprises, which is fine as long as I don't have a deadline or a particular destination in mind. Radio waves of a certain frequency bounce off the ionosphere, while others scatter when they hit walls and bodies. A few slide between layers of the troposphere, ducting their way from California to Hawaii on a clear day. Still, they arrive, echoing and chaotic, landing but approximately where aimed. I can manage the same on the best of days.

Circling the campus for an hour, the morning sun burning its dreadfulness into my eyes, I try to avoid turning students into speed bumps and demolition-*derbying* my way through the overcrowded streets. I grumble the entire time, first good-naturedly, later, with frustration, my floridly vulgar tirade carrying outside the thin-walled cabin of my 1998 Tacoma.

The time comes and goes, and I give up—another failed trip, another signal absorbed by an ionosphere overexcited by light—returning to my brother's cabin, where I have been staying for the last two days, my annoyance settling into gentle resignation. If nothing else, the misadventure reaffirms my decision to never again set foot (or tire) on university grounds and avoid their hilly one-way lanes.

***

I don't delete the recruitment email—an unusual choice for me. With few exceptions, I keep only what I need. Nor does the email delete itself, so it sits on the server and in the back of my consciousness.

A month after my missed meeting, I send a reply: *Are there any positions still available? I missed the open house.* What I receive in return is a phone number and a request to call on an upcoming Tuesday.

The woman who answers my call is obviously Chinese. Her English is fine, if heavily accented with a country-song-melodic mixture of Mandarin tonality and Southern twang, and she is busy—too busy to talk to me, it seems. *Yes, there are still open positions. But you must hurry. Call my colleague in Atlanta for details.*

But you must hurry is less than entirely true. In the late aughts, China is hiring everyone with a pulse, a White face, and a semi-credible Photoshopped scan of a degree. This xenomania occurs from time to time in the Middle Kingdom, but briefly and according to a broadly predictable cycle: China opens (*fang*) for a decade or two, then closes (*shou*), often abruptly, and this is the peak of China's inviting era. Tighter standards, better background checks, and mass departures of foreigners are not far beyond the horizon. By the time COVID hits more than a decade later, not many foreigners will be left to flee the endless rounds of nasal swabs and lockdowns—with those absurdities striking the final, merciful death blow to China's *laowai* population and sending the most firm-gripped of old hands, some with decades of experience in-country, elsewhere, and turning exclaves of big-nosed foreignness into ghost towns.

But that's all in the future.

No one tells me as much, but obtaining a Chinese contract and a visa are formalities circa 2009. The job offer—*to teach what? And how without knowing any Chinese?*—is itself something I still regard with suspicion. Nevertheless, I make another call. And this time, an American answers.

Older than I am in the aughts (but probably still in his thirties), the man—Bill—is energetic and overamped, with a hint of desperate enthusiasm in his voice. Later, when I start a recruitment firm of my own—*Ganbei Teach and Travel* (slogan: *Drink to teach! Teach to Drink!*)—I will come to see the extraordinary fickleness of job candidates. A reluctance to travel (although they applied for an overseas job), a suspicion of everything and everyone, and a fixation on random, shiny things (a consternating question on a medical form or a need to book a flight 27.5 days ahead of time)—these were *some* of the more peculiar traits of the motley crew of the White faces drawn to China at the end of Hu Jintao's tenure.

Thus, Bill's rapid-fire pitch is practical—trying to get me to sign on the dotted line before I back out, hoping to keep me engaged enough to follow through from there.

Rattling off contending cities, the Atlantan pitches them on their respective strengths, doing his best to draw an image of vibrancy, of an ever-increasing dynamism. He is but moderately successful, yet despite my being more consternated than not, I manage a question: *What's the least touristy place you know? Can you send me somewhere authentic?* He pauses.

Well, there's always Huaihua.

***

Between my home in Kentucky and the ATL, the meaning of *authentic* undergoes one metamorphosis, if not many. Such is another miracle of distance. I mean *natural; true to the character of the place*, whereas what Bill hears is *somewhere no one in his right mind would go; possibly uninhabitable by foreigners; in proximity to a large cache of nuclear warheads*.

The nuclear warheads are to prove more of a point of interest than anything else, which is to say none of them are tested on me, nor am I asked to operate them. But watching the soldiers walk by me on the permanently under-construction streets, their unit patches emblazoned with the insignia of the PLA Rocket Force—a red-tipped, white missile surrounded by gold laurels—I will come to realize how vast the expanse is between *here* and home. Although the mission of the men of Base 55 (the headquarters of which I am destined to walk past several times a day) is to obliterate Guam at a moment's notice, the threatened violence is singularly impersonal, with no one giving me so much as a dirty look. Come the first cold spell in China, I will buy a PLA surplus greatcoat, oversized and ill-fitting. The coat's hard olive canvas shell will haltingly move with my body as I wade through the drizzle from one campus to the next, and the soldiers, for all their spit-and-polish and shiny black boots, will invariably, if briefly, do a double-take and grin before returning to their studied impassiveness.

But that's all later.

The same remoteness that makes Huaihua impenetrable to enemy land forces gives it exactly what I have requested—*authenticity*. Nestled between the Wuling and Xuefeng Mountain ranges, there are three ways into (or out of) the city: a rail line, a recently completed arterial road, and Zhijiang Airport, which is some 30 kilometers from the city center and the PLA base HQ. The first two go through long mountain tunnels, supposedly rigged with explosives for quick closure. The last was formerly a military installation and is easily defended or demolished.

Notwithstanding the craggy terrain surrounding it, the city has an abundance of food. The rich black soil can grow everything from rice to clementines to fruits and vegetables unknown to me before leaving the States. Hothouse summers and soggy, miserable winters, while uncomfortable for man and beast, make for a paradise for flora. In the warmer months, plants grow and blossom with a frenetic intensity, and the cooler months are never cold enough to kill the least cold-hardy perennials—peppers first amongst them—allowing them to yield two harvests a year. That, combined with the nearby power plant, gives the city a particular resilience, letting it stand apart from the rest of the country. Huaihua, much like Kentucky, is an especially good place to weather the end of the world (even if it might play an integral part in said end), not solely because of its resources and well-constructed autonomy, but because everything happens 20 years later here.

***

Huaihua's distinctive charm reveals itself slowly—one of those rugged faces that is never quite handsome but wins you over with its smile. At first, the sidewalks, lined with hole-in-the-wall restaurants and little family stores that sold cup noodles and Nongfu Springs drinks, overwhelm me—there's too much new to process.

The place is ancient, sort of. Humans have lived here for twenty-eight millennia or more, with Miao, Tujia, and Han settling in waves, each leaving mementoes of their industriousness—bronze and iron tools, pottery and artwork, rice grains and stone carvings—buried in the caves and loamy fields, before eventually blending into a cohesive people.

But *the city is new*. Its craggy terrain and terraced fields didn't surrender to modernity until Mao's sent-down youths and railway gangs tunneled through the mountains and laid the steel of the Xiangqian line atop the fragrant corpse of the old Hehuang Culture.

So Huaihua is equal parts iron and steel, jade and plastic.

Welders scattered about, goggle-less and plying their trade on the sidewalk, fabricate security bars for the complexes rising as fast from the oilseed fields as giant grasses from the hills. And the constant honking, thumping, two-stroke disorder of the roads and the jackhammering of demolition crews contribute to the sense that Huaihua is under both construction and *destruction*. With each herky-jerky lurch towards modernity and prehistoric, ragged breath, the city is building itself up as it shakes itself apart, and the traffic is one collision away from a chain reaction of relativistic-velocity neutrons and *Final Destination*-caliber vehicular carnage.

Yet it doesn't. There is no *boom* or catastrophic crash. Huaihua grows faster than it can fall.

However much I try to ignore it—to regard it as background hum, a part of the character of the place and acoustic static—the constant thrum-rattle-beep keeps me on edge for months.

I grew up surrounded by alfalfa and empty stables—my ears calibrated to the rustling of the silage crops and Queen Anne's lace with every gust and breeze through the valley of the low fields below my family's tumbledown, faintly moldy 70s split-level. So there was no easy way to adjust and mentally squelch the noise below a set threshold. Back on the farm, amongst the rot, one could very nearly hear the mushrooms sprouting from the decaying basement carpet. But in the pearl-gray light of early morning, the din and rumble of Huaihua and her trains are forever present, if muted.

I gradually absorb the noise, and the fine and sporadically present tremors in my hands come to fall on the beat of Huaihua's pulse. Upon returning to the States, the assertion of my students who travelled there—that the country is *too quiet*—will *click*, though I may never agree with it.

***

For all the noise, the most jarring thing about Huaihua is that my supervisors appear no less ignorant of my purpose than I am.

My first week in China suggests that no one knows what to do with me. Nashville, Houston, Los Angeles, Beijing, then Changsha—my trip is uneventful, save for the nerves I have along the way. Preparation for the trip was trivial. All I own of value is my Tacoma, which I leave at my father's house and which he promises to start from time to time in my absence, and all I take with me is a grade-school-sized backpack filled with clothes and a book. My reading material—the *Pocket Oxford American Dictionary & Thesaurus*—turns out to be a poor choice. Neither engaging enough to distract me nor boring enough to allow me to calm my nagging anxiety, the *Oxford* becomes a peculiar source of comfort, nonetheless. It serves as something to hold onto as I pass through immigration. And it's something to thumb through as I sit down for my first drink in 14 hours—a Fanta bought at a Jackie Chan-themed (and presumably licensed) drink stand (*or* restaurant *or* my-memory-fails-me-but-I-know-it-had-something-to-do-with-Jackie establishment) at the shiny-new and pristine Beijing Capital Airport.

I hold it firmly when I walk off the plane in Changsha, where I am greeted by one of my recruiters' daughters—a cheerful teenager with clipped English and a fascination with Eminem—her driver, and a wall of soul-draining humidity that would put the hottest Kentucky August to shame. The teenager, for all her bubbly charm and assistance with my single backpack of luggage, can do little to answer my questions, knowing that we would go *somewhere to meet someone*, presumably Chinese, who would escort me from there, but nothing else.

The *somewhere* I meet the school representative is an open market—equal parts stalls and street carts. Such places are ubiquitous in China circa 2009, but no less confounding to me than an Aztec temple would have been to a travel-worn conquistador. The representative, *Lawrence* (his English name), is stocky, friendly, and miraculously and majestically calm given his unrelenting intake of squat golden cans of Thai Red Bull, Baisha cigarettes, and betel nut husks (*bīng kē* in Mandarin, *bing na* in *Huaihua-ese*). His track wear—Nike sneakers, jacket, and pants from head to toe—seems a bold choice for a stocky chain smoker. But I might be underestimating the power of fitness apparel in China, which could, presumably, make one fit simply by donning it.

The point where I clutch my Oxford harder still is when Lawrence guides me under the market to a parking garage. This is a cavern of fumes and shadows so sinister I brace to thwack, thrash, and grammatically correct a flock (or *murder?*) of organ dealers, each vying for my kidneys, virginal—as they are—from the effects of Chinese sorghum liquor and recycled cooking oil.

Lawrence, knowing nothing of my suspicions, loiters around a manager's office and stuffs in a second and third *bīng kē*. In due time, we're loaded onto a minibus that skates over a glass-smooth highway past a blur of undifferentiated green and the occasional gas station, then dropped in the knotted traffic of Huaihua's disordered central boulevard. From there, we take a taxi to the university.

***

That's where I sit—on the tree-lined campus of China's 500th (or so) best university, in a nearly bare apartment with a broken-down sofa, a box spring without mattress or sheets, and a leaking water cooler on an entertainment desk next to an unplugged CRT. Not wanting to pester my neighbors more than I must, I keep my perplexity largely to myself. Lawrence helps me get a phone—an unlicensed copy of an already bargain-basement Chinese candy bar—and I commandeer a dusty computer from an unoccupied ground-floor unit. With some cursing and struggle, I manage to connect to the internet. This seems as much as I can reasonably expect, so I find small amusements where I can.

Thus far, I have received no assignments, instructions, or explanation of my role. I begin to wonder if my purpose is simply to exist—to sit in my apartment, fill a quota, and warm a chair. Or I might have been forgotten, lost in a stack of paperwork in a language I cannot read.

I spend my considerable free time walking around campus, which is proving fascinating, if more befuddling than elucidating. The centerpiece of this collection of squat buildings with crumbling stucco is an under-landscaped park featuring a moon goddess statue, never occupied benches, and a bone-dry fountain. More curiously, another park, far removed from the other, is hidden atop a hill amongst abandoned low-rises and badly overgrown with weeds, and accessible by a spiral steel staircase. Only its ornately decorated pavilion, with flying eaves and an interlocking phoenix-and-dragon painted on its ceiling, hints that the place had ever received more than cursory attention.

More curious still is the concrete basketball court I pass through on my way to the campus's blocky gate, clad in red tiles, with gold calligraphy running the length of its lintel. Nearly empty upon my arrival, the court is flooded one morning with hundreds of training soldiers. For all my martial ignorance, I spot irregularities: not all the uniforms match. Some recruits wear blue-black-gray camouflage, its chocolate-chip spots reworked for the open sea. (I have yet to grasp why one would *want* overboard sailors to disappear into the ocean—unless to make rescue impossible and save on recovery costs—but I digress.) Others wear a near-clone of the U.S. Woodland pattern, better suited to the local terrain's brown soil and emerald foliage. The troops—*recruits, militiamen, who knows?*—have neither insignia nor name tape, nor apparent access to firearms, nor wooden replicas of the same. Is this school a military academy? Would I have been told?

My neighbor is unsure of the reason for the sudden militarization of the campus. I would ask a Chinese, but I know just one, and he—Lawrence—disappeared after helping me buy a phone. And I believe it's best not to pry too aggressively into what might be a matter of national defense or pride. I steer clear of the soldiers/recruits/mountain rangers, lest I am wrong about the absence of weapons and my pale face ends up on the wrong side of a well-aimed fusillade.

When not ambling about, I think about food, which, for the first week, consists of spicy peanuts and soft drinks, and is becoming an issue. My long-term vegetarianism and a stomach that balks at the safest day's offering of canned soup and boiled noodles make me cautious of anything I could order from the neighboring dives. The school canteen, with its indecipherable signage and cooks wielding cleavers with a manic, furious precision (the sight of which causes me to suspect I might lose a finger or three if I were less than a meter away), offers prospects but uncertainly better. So, peanuts, plain chips, and Fanta appear to be the extent of foolproof menu options for some time to come.

Knock! Knock! Knock!

I look up from my computer screen to the paper-thin door and the lock that works when so inclined, which is not often.

Who would that be?

I am expecting no one and have no reason to think anyone had any business with me.

"Hello!"

I can hear the Chinese from the first syllable.

Lawrence? But why?

Knock! Knock! Knock!

I get up. I open the door.

"Are you the American?"

Before me stands a Chinese man, no more than 20 years of age, with rough skin and narrow glasses resting atop his unusually broad nose. (I would add that he had cropped dark hair, but after a week in China, I realize that part of the description is can nearly be taken for granted.)

"Well," I think, turning the object of the sentence—*the American*—around for a moment (*Are there others? Does my Americanness mean something in particular?*), "I, I suppose so."

"I'm Ethan. Consider me the *welcome wagon*," And he invites himself in.

Ethan looks around the apartment, "I see your apartment is ... furnished." I catch the careful choice of words. Ethan sounds underwhelmed. He scowls the way Chinese do—quickly, without much flourish, the expression centered around the eyes.

"Pleasure to meet you, Ethan, I'm Brant Goble," I answer. He continues his inspection, my words not slowing him down at all. I don't know if I should be annoyed. *Is this the way the*

Chinese do things? Does everyone wander in as they please?
"May I help you with something? Are you from the school?"

"I'm a student from the Economics Department." And into the kitchen he goes. I hope the cockroaches—*the other tenants*, I christen them (before I come to realize their real utility)—have the good grace to scatter across the dingy white subway tiles and hide. "How long have you been here?"

"Not long, not much more than a week."

"Do you need any help with anything? Are you adjusting to life here?"

"Well, I suppose, all is well. But if you don't mind me asking, do you know where I can buy food?"

Ethan opens the refrigerator. "Oh! Nothing! I see you have nothing!" Ethan *tut-tuts*, "I would have thought the school would have sent someone to escort you to a supermarket."

"That would have been nice!"

But *nice* is not something I can expect. No matter how long I work in education, how many awards I earn, or how many credentials I complete, I will never be paid much attention by my employers, be they Chinese, Georgian, or Hungarian. Delayed wages, a total lack of help with immigration, and emails left unanswered for weeks—these will be the order of the day for years, until I become a far less pleasant person. I have a forgettable face, I suppose, and shaking off my softened, Southern, harmless delivery and apologetic phrasing will prove not much less challenging than learning to distinguish the four tones of Mandarin.

***

Jiawei Supermarket is not far from campus, but its location is poorly marked. It—like the parking garage in which I feared the proletariat would appropriate my kidneys—is underground. This is something I will come to notice about China: the store buried under the store, the restaurant beneath the roundabout, and the discount phone seller accessible by descending through an unlit tunnel and a rickety flight of wooden stairs. The cities here are stacked high and low.

The ride to Jiawei is an adventure, with a blue-uniformed driver whose gear shifts result in a clunk-bang-whine so intense that I believe he harbors a deep generational antipathy towards the bus's transmission. His slamming through lights and veering in and out of lanes with a speed that would be difficult in a Porsche adds to the thrill. More wondrous still is that he manages this with a bus so overstuffed with passengers (and with but a limited number of seats for the aged and pregnant) that every turn and bounce slams sweating bodies into each other, nearly knocking them off their feet as they ride the waves of diesel smoke and melting rubber to what one fears is their *Final Destination*.

The supermarket's interior, aside from the Chinese characters and jewelry counter selling jade, is not much different from stores at home. Ethan patiently reads the food labels, translating for me as he goes.

He seems undisturbed by the ā yí—aunties, middle-aged women—who push past him in the aisles.

"Can you eat yams? Or noodles? Or noodles made from yams?"

"Sure! Yes to all three."

"Can you eat something that contains," he stares at the label, mutters, and checks the terms on his phone's dictionary, "monosodium glutamate and disodium guanylate."

Now, *I* am the one who pauses.

"That should be fine… I think."

***

One more *Fast & Furious: Hunan Bus Drift* ride back to campus, and we are in my apartment after I stop by the ATM to withdraw another stack of red 100-yuan notes. Ethan helps me put away my food. I have noodles, rice, some vegetables that I assume can be boiled and mashed, and snacks I am eager to try. I have a rice cooker as well, and Ethan explains its proper use in some detail. I also have tea—loose-leaf green with jasmine—which Ethan shows me how to make in the Chinese manner: take a tiny, extraordinarily fragile plastic cup, add a pinch of tea leaves, and pour in scalding hot water from the recently upgraded (non-leaking) water dispenser. Now, hold the deforming plastic cup by its supremely thin lip, and take a sip of the tea, enjoying the permanent thermal damage to your tongue with every drink.

I have questions about the safety and efficacy of this method, but interrogating Ethan after his hours of help rings of disrespect. We exchange phone numbers, and he is out the door as quickly as he appeared.

I still have no idea why Ethan helped me.

***

Guests begin arriving with increasing frequency—some considerate, some curious, and some wanting to practice their English—usually limited—before nodding and wandering away. There are other outsiders here—my British neighbor, a teacher from Africa, and some Ukrainian students in another complex—but none have the obvious draw of an American. Or it might be that no other foreigner is willing to open his door and entertain guests whenever they appear.

Either way, after weeks on campus, I have been given no portfolio, and getting to know the student body seems as good a use of time as any. I am learning as I go—suitable restaurants and orders, the names and functions of a few buildings, and where on campus to buy daily necessities. I have also picked up a handful of Chinese characters, enough to recognize the words for meat (which I avoid) and milk (which I avoid no less diligently).

***

Knock! Knock!

These knocks are light, and two rather than three. *Hmm?* Ethan usually texts before he appears.

"Hello, my friend. Are you home?"

This voice is female, definitely Chinese, and *loud. My friend? How many friends do I have here?*

I roll out of bed and dress, buttoning my shirt and tucking it into my oversized jeans with as much care as I can muster at this hour.

"Hello, friend! Are you there?" I can hear her through the door, every syllable clear, filled with effervescence.

Impatient! But I slouch ever closer to the door, which I open, proffering my wan, too-early-for-this smile, and before me stands a student with a broad smile on her face and a twinkle in her eye. It occurs to me my hair remains unbrushed—not *I-spent-15-years-in-a-private-prison* messy, but hardly *I'm-the-guy-who-imprisoned-you-for-15-years* tidy either.

"Good morning! Were you in bed?"

I glance down at my recently purchased Casio F91W—the preferred watch of underpaid teachers, schoolchildren, cabdrivers, and *alleged* al-Qaeda members (often poor schlub cabdrivers picked up by bounty hunters and sold to U.S. forces in Afghanistan).

"It is eight o'clock." *Do I know this woman?*

"Yes," I hesitate, uncertain of how to respond to this declaration, "it is."

"May I come in?" *Well, at least she asked.*

At this point, I have learned something of Chinese manners, so I offer *unnamed probable friend* a cup of torture tea—scalding hot and in the customary microns-thin, uninsulated cup. I have no idea what to call this young woman with her flowery shirt and unlikely morning sparkle-spirit, and my skill at distinguishing Chinese faces, while improving, is less than optimal. Learning to see past similarities and recognize the subtle differences within a population takes time. I wonder if I look like every other White guy on the planet to my guests. Could I pass for a *Seven*-era Brad Pitt? A *Dr. No*-decade Sean Connery (whom my young guests would likely be unable to recognize)?

"Nice to see you," I collect my thoughts for a moment, "*friend*, what can I do for you?"

She sits down, and I pass her tea to her, trying to avoid pouring it into her lap. I make myself an instant coffee.

"You do not know me!" she chuckles as she says it, and I am relieved I can stop trying to remember a name I never knew. "I am Mei, but you can call me Lily. I would like to interview you."

"Now?" *About what?*

"No, next week. We can meet at the East Campus. So will you do it?"

"As opposed to the ... Which campus is this?" I point to the floor. *Another chuckle.*

"This is the West Campus! And in the meantime, do you need any help?"

"Sure, and sure, I suppose. I do have questions."

"Shoot!"

Which leads to my more-or-less-aimed volley of interrogatives and the heartening realization that I am not, in fact, about to be *shot*.

Better yet, I am told that the mass of *soldiers* who had appeared on and then disappeared from the basketball court were not professional fighters at all, but rather first-year students undergoing the Chinese version of reserve officer training. Their training, which also serves as a team-building exercise of sorts (with students assigned to small teams from their academic department), consists primarily of running, push-ups, pull-ups, and marching in formation. Lily is quite firm that no one—herself included—had so much as fired a rifle, much less at the silhouette of a pale-faced outsider.

Lily provides still more information, including insights into the disordered mechanics of the college's administration—a system with which she is greatly displeased. I am beginning to develop a better understanding of how this place operates: The leadership being incommunicado (aside from helping me buy a phone) is not personal, but an accepted practice. And Lily's explanations are entertaining, and with her alternating near-yell and stage whispers, I get the sense we are gossiping about people I have never met.

As has become custom, Lily and I exchange numbers. I confirm my willingness to be interviewed (*about what*, I have no idea), and Lily turns to leave. She stops.

"By the way, what is your name, dear teacher?"

"Oh! Brant Goble."

"See you soon, Teacher Goble!"

And Lily departs, no less enthusiastic than she was upon her arrival.

***

As much as I enjoy my random assortment of guests, I am glad for the days I am left unbothered. My computer works (more or less), and the Great Firewall of China has yet to be built so high that it blocks much access to the outside world: I can still send emails and read the news easily enough. I begin to draft an essay—nothing interesting, nothing with much insight, to fight the weakness of my ever-collapsing memory—to memorialize the novelty of my circumstances. *Teacher Goble must keep himself busy until he has someone (and something) to teach.*

***

"Where are you? We have class today!" *He's annoyed.*

I lift my head from my pillow and pull back the phone, considering the time and date on the screen.

"Good to hear from you, Lawrence! Today is Sunday, you know, and what classes?"

"We are starting the semester early because of the holiday." I would ask *what holiday*, but Lawrence sounds overwrought—for him, which is to say I am inclined to believe he is not about to drift off in the course of our conversation. I think I can hear him spit out a chewed-up betel husk. *Is that what he does when upset? Part camel, I suppose. Pity he doesn't have nicer eyelashes.*

"You must come to the Dean's office."

"Where is that?"

"The English Building," he's calmer now, regaining his patience. *Sigh.*

"Where is that?"

"The East Campus!"

"And where is that?"

"East of you!"

Lawrence is about as agitated as I can imagine his phlegmatic person becoming. And I am beginning to fear I may give him a heart attack. For liability reasons, I decide I will shift the blame to the cigarettes and Red Bull—the manufacturers likely have deeper pockets to boot.

"So, I just start walking east, Lawrence?" *Ah, that might be it! Finally, an adventure.*

Lawrence doesn't immediately reply. I think I can hear him opening another can of Thai miracle juice.

"Do you know where the gate is?"

"The red thing with the Chinese words on top?"

"Exactly! Go there. Wait for the shuttle."

***

After the shuttle deposits me under a concrete-and-sheet-metal porte-cochere in front of a building faced with the ubiquitous subway tiles—these in putty pink and dirty off-white—I shamble about for a half-dozen minutes, death-gripping my thermos of Nescafé and scratching my unwashed head. The trip was refreshingly gentle, in a well-appointed bus driven by a man who, unlike his city-bus counterparts, was not vying to star in the Hong Kong remake of *Bullitt*.

A student, noticing my directionless wanderings, volunteers as a guide and walks me from a rarely used bank of payphones to the English Building and up the six flights of stairs to the Dean's office.

The Dean, a rail-thin woman in a power suit in muted brown, with the hollows under her eyes of the permanently sleep-deprived, narrows her expression.

"You are late. Today is photo day, and why are you not teaching?"

"Teaching what?"—*this being the question I have wanted to ask for the last several weeks.*

"Your classes. You have class today." I look around at the harsh light of the unadorned office. Lawrence, standing behind me, appears to think the scolding applies to him as well.

"I understand." *I don't but...*

"Here is your schedule. Since you have been late *again*, perhaps you could teach an English corner as well." I'm about to point out that my apartment already is an English practice center (if not an actual corner) for all who knock, but the Dean's *again* stops me. I look down at the paper written in Chinese.

"I can't read this."

Lawrence, sheepish before his superior, gently takes the paper from me and inspects it.

"Oh, sorry!" and he scribbles the days of the week across the top row. "These are the room numbers." He taps the boxes below. "And the time is here—" his pen sweeps the leftmost column of 45-minute blocks in military time.

I'm glad for the last point—I'm familiar with the 24-hour clock from my amateur radio days—so I know not to show up at two in the morning.

"Great! What do I do today?"

"Nothing, you start tomorrow," the Dour Dean waits a beat, "You missed your lessons."

"Then, I suppose I will see everyone on Monday." I exit, bowing a bit, before the Dour Dean's displeasure has time to burn a hole through my skin.

***

Monday comes, and I am standing behind a particleboard desk in a classroom on the eighth floor. I can feel my stomach gurgling and churning with black coffee and anxiety. Walking through the drizzle from the aforementioned porte-cochere (which I was told minutes prior is attached to the Computer Science Building) to the English Building's overhang, I absorbed exactly the requisite moisture for optimal discomfort—feeling both clammy and steamily overcooked, depending on the body part. To its credit, the rain broke the summer heat, and the classroom, while not comfortable, is not sweltering.

The students, parked behind long benches with wooden tip-up seats, are bright-eyed and attentive, if exceptionally reticent to speak. Of the approximately 35 students, all but two are young women. This is the average ratio, and in the following four years of teaching, I will never see a class in the English department with more than 15% men.

Further pushing down the noise floor is the complete absence of electricity—no fluorescent hum, no whirring fans, no clicking electronics. Light, to the extent it is provided, comes through a wall of south-facing windows that are also the room's sole means of ventilation, and the dull gray-weather wash that trickles through strips the room of color.

I can hear myself breathe. Smartphones will not be ubiquitous for another year or two. The dumbphones that some (not all) of the students have are good for not much more than calls, messaging paramours and parents, and the occasional game of snakes—none of which are likely to appeal much at this early hour.

There is but one instructional tool in the classroom—a chalkboard, which would be fine had someone advised me of the school's *bring-your-own-chalk* (BYOC) policy and told me where to purchase said chalk. *But they did not tell, and I did not ask, so here we are.* My grandmother, who began her teaching career during the Second World War in the Appalachian foothills, had slightly more resources at her disposal.

All I have at mine is my decidedly un-mellifluous voice and a limited capacity to charm.

"Good morning, all! My name is Brant Goble, and today," I panic for a moment—*What subject is this?*—remembering that Dour Dean never told me the name of the course. *Ah! I have it!* "We will be introducing ourselves! When I ask you to stand, please give me your name, reason for attending college, and something you would like the class to know about you." "You there—the young lady in the red coat—let's start with you." *Someone laughs. Is "lady" offensive here? Anyway...*

One by one, the students stand and announce their names—unpronounceable to me—their career goals (all aiming for teaching or international trade), and more often than not, their hometowns and a fact about their background.

This time-killing exercise proves more fruitful than I anticipated. Most of my students are from the smallest of communities, first-generation college students, and (as far as I can tell) absolutely sincere in their desire to study and learn. The more I hear and the more closely I observe them, the more I recognize certain ruralisms we share that, despite differences in cultural context, translate well enough—the modest dress, the careful etiquette, and the lack of city-folk cynicism.

There are few people more careful in their behavior than those of modest countryside upbringings who aspire to improve themselves and their lot through sheer studiousness. They wear their education, their manners, and cultivation carefully—a well-made coat they worked hard for years to buy and cannot afford to replace if torn. We are quietly proud of our finery, even though donning it feels vaguely absurd. For them, no less than for me, refinement is a fragile thing—hard-won, likely to be stolen away, with our spirits left haunting the city square.

The *securely prosperous* have the luxury of mistakes and youthful folly—crashed cars and unrecorded abortions. The *resignedly poor* have little concern for the opinions of polite company, with some of the more refractory relishing their own crassness and ability to offend. But the *born-bumpkin-become-better* is a careful outsider, no longer at home amongst the hayseeds and hokeyness, but rarely with the quick, self-assured brashness of urbanites born to the glaring lights, grand towers, and *prestissimo* tempo of a life of constant flow and hustle. These are the people who struggle to keep up appearances in word, deed, and presentation, through every misfortune and disaster as though the veneer of respectability—of civilization—might crack if dropped or jostled hard.

They might well be right.

Almost none of the students have met a foreigner before, and with one or two exceptions, I am the first American they have seen. As class winds down, I open the floor to questions about me, which proves invaluable. Just as the students' introductions allowed me to better understand them, their questions give me an idea of how I am likely to be perceived: a curiosity, with the most significant curiosity being why an American would choose to live in Huaihua and teach at a school where chalk, much like honor, is earned, never given.

This—*Why are you here?*—and the somewhat less directly asked (but often implied) question— *Why is an American here?*—is one I will be asked throughout my travels, with the subtext being that anyone from the United States should bounce exclusively from one first-tier city to the next.

***

On the smooth shuttle ride back to my apartment, I watch the new constructions roll by through a rain-streaked window and consider my situation: I have no assigned subject or portfolio. And after weeks of being ignored by Lawrence (and Dour Dean's subsequent irked welcome), I am hopeful my relationship with the leadership will be a distant one. I have a blank slate—a board as clean as the one on which I had no chalk to write.

This suits me perfectly.

My master's degree has been dead in the water for a semester. My coursework is complete, but I have made no progress on the research and teaching components, mainly because, despite living in Kentucky for most of my life, I know of no organization where I could be placed and have no contacts to help me find one.

Growing up, I thought of home primarily in terms of *infrastructure*—power, water, roads, and access to the postal system. I have no experiences of trauma, no tales of abuse or being stuffed into a locker, no scars or tears from the blanked-out terror of homophobic rednecks doing *androphilic* things to me in showers. I have never been abused, and I harbor no ill will towards the place where I was raised. The negligible number of negative memories I have are of no consequence. More relevant is the lack of positive ones.

My connections to the farm, the countryside, and the culture, much like my nationality, were never much more than accidents of birth. *I am from nowhere.* But of course, there is no *nowhere*—everywhere is somewhere. Every place has its stories, but those of Kentucky never felt like mine. My rustic memories are of a liminal place—no moonshine, no hell-raising, no country boy pride (or shame, for that matter). Although I knew the occasional character steeped in rebel-flag, South-will-rise-again identity, they were the most distant of acquaintances. One can live two doors down (or 100 acres away) from another—in the same county—yet be a world away. My countryside, *my* little non-place, was another *somewhere* the wind blew through on the way to *somewhere else*, a patch of grass in the night where starlight landed and died.

At best, the stories and associations of Kentucky are incidental—a title to a plot on the moon, somehow mine, through gift or inheritance, but irrelevant. On my darker days, I imagined my spirit being that of cheap wine—no *terroir*—a jug handle and sketch of a smiling man standing in front of distant vineyards.

I have long been sensitive to this—if not quite self-conscious—of the nondescriptness of me and mine, and that it left me lacking. This deficiency of color and distinctness—that sense of *voidness*, of coming from a sterile, lifeless place defined by where it is not—is what made travel, to China in particular, so very appealing. More positively, it made travel easy: Leaving *somewhere* is difficult. Leaving *nowhere* is no trouble at all. Why be sentimental?

From my shortwave days, I wanted to go somewhere *in particular*—a place with a memorable style and flavor and unique soil and sun of its own. On long, nippy autumn nights spent hunched over my Sangean, I'd listen to the blaring horns of Radio Havana or the cheerfully singsong English of Radio Taiwan. I'd think of the signals and how they landed in places beyond the humming power lines, the rush of wind through the grasses, and the unceasing low roar of gravel crushers from the nearby quarry. And I wished I could magic-carpet them elsewhere.

Hence, *authentic* Huaihua.

Now that I am *somewhere*, I need a plan—what to teach and how to tie it to my degree. Letting myself into my apartment, I remove my wet socks and drooping jacket. I sniff. They both smell of damp dog. *I don't have a dog, so the wet dog must be me.*

I make a cup of torture tea—pain focuses the mind—and scoop rice into the cooker's pot, washing it until the water poured off is clear. *What to teach? What to teach?* I mutter. I turn on the cooker, the timer snapping into place loudly enough to scare away the cockroaches.

What to teach? What to teach? I wash and peel the sweet potatoes, preparing them for boiling. The Hunanese stir-fry most of what they eat and steam the rest, the latter including various breads and stuffed buns. Boiled food is not verboten—there is rice congee and hot pot (though I would argue the boiling broth therein is used to scald rather than properly cook). But my students would likely consider a meal of boiled roots and vegetables as punishment for a bad grade. *Of course, I am not them, and they are not me.* To the extent that I have any certainty about my ancestry, I know that some of it is English: terrible food is a tradition. I wonder if my English neighbor is also ruining the local produce.

My degrees—a finished bachelor's in management, and my uncompleted master's in adult education—offer little guidance. *What do I know that my students need to know?* Thinking back to the Spartan resources of the classroom, another question pops into my head: *What can I teach without non-existent textbooks, intermittent electricity, and as much chalk as I can carry in my duffle bag?*

And, just as importantly, what do the students want to learn?

Then the answer occurs to me as I drop sweet potatoes into a pot:

Back in my community college days, I took a required public speaking course, and therein is my template.

I had no talent for public performance, with my highlight presentation (to the extent I had one) entailing bringing a two-dollar rubber snake to class with the professor's amused permission and giving an underwhelming presentation on George Went Hensley. Hensley—the minister who founded the Church of God with Signs Following (and maybe/possibly/probably-not distant relative)—handled serpents as a demonstration of his trust in the Lord. While I could never relate to such dazzling recklessness and absolute faith in the unseen and unseeable—the very concept alienating me—George proved a worthwhile subject. And his faith served *me* well: I passed the class.

Which is not to say it ultimately did George much good.

Whereas George eventually succumbed to his diminishing conviction (and subsequent anaphylaxis), mine—mine, regarding what to teach, if nothing else—grows.

No books? No problem?

No projector or PowerPoint? No problem?

No electricity? No problem!

All I need is a syllabus, which I can cobble together easily. My oratorical incompetence should prove no obstacle—*those who can't, teach*. And the students would be doing more talking than I would.

Now, there is the matter of how to tie this to my master's.

***

I wing my way through the first week of classes—introductions and a chance for them to question me if time permits—following my first day's template. When the lights turn on mid-class on Wednesday (after I have started outlining my course), I take it as a sign that my plan, if not blessed by whatever higher power has jurisdiction over scribbling sages, snakebites, and syllabi in Hunan, is under favorable review.

So I suppose I have a faith of my own.

For manifold reasons, my class will not be a carbon copy of the one I took in community college.

First, I have no textbook at my disposal and no recollection of which textbook was used. Second, I think the original course—designed for older American students with full-time jobs, life experiences, and a working man's jaundiced eye—is, for lack of a better description, *too dry* for bright-eyed and bushy-tailed charges. So, I add extra projects for levity—a mock trial and a business presentation, along with quick quizzes and simple games.

I've already observed enough in my first week to realize that these young people, with infrequent exceptions, are more fluent than they believe and more dedicated than their American counterparts. And their halting and hesitation are more issues of confidence than competence. *I think I can fix this, and doing so might be fun.*

In an email to my professor—a man I have never met and whose voice I have heard once—I explain where I am and that I aim to complete my teaching practicum this semester and attach a draft syllabus. I present this as *fate accompli*—a calculated risk, but from what I have ascertained from my professor's hem-and-haw phrasings and cautious (if polite) noncommittalism, likely the best approach. *Better to ask forgiveness than permission*. By the weekend, I have a syllabus, a plan for completing my teaching practicum, and sufficient familiarity with Chinese snacks and vegetables to go shopping without a minder.

***

Knock! Knock! Knock!

"Hello! Hello!" *Lily?* "I know you are there, Dear Teacher! When are you going to open the door?"

I have no reason to anticipate Lily's appearance on this cloudless Sunday afternoon. We had completed our interview—a polite affair held in the miniature park in front of the English Building days ago—and it seemed to have gone well enough. Sitting on squat concrete stools in front of a pond and a recently installed stone bridge, she asked me the same questions as had everyone else—*Why are you in China? What brought you to Huaihua? How is China different from America? What do you think of the food? Are Chinese people friendly?*—but in a radio voice of such astounding effervescence and vigor (and that compared to her standard preternatural enthusiasm) that I weighed the answers with care, uncertain of the extent of my commitment. *Should I buy Amway from her, or agree to sign over my assets to the temple?*

I like Lily, admiring her can-do mindset and her unabashed energy, but after no more than a week in Hunan, I appreciate that she is not on the same frequency as her peers, and she modulates her message differently. Big, bold, and occasionally staticky, Lily has all the subtlety of a Mexican megawatt border blaster. The other students (with few exceptions) rely far more on subtle methods, and I have a lingering suspicion that Lily's bouncing outdoor-loud energy will put her at odds with some of her peers, if it hasn't yet done so.

After our interview ended, the recorder off, Lily leaned in close, *sotto voce*—meaning no one more than five meters away could hear—confessing that she intended to change her major from business to English. This, she explained, was the most *Schwarzenegger-ean* of Herculean efforts, requiring many different signatures and seals of approval. Our conversations had inspired her, and my boldness was her motivation.

Oh dear.

"Hello! Hello!" I hear the sunshine-cheer threatening to burn a hole in my door.

And as is custom at the *Grand Château de Goblé et sa fidèle garde d'insectes*, Lily brushes past me once I open the door and into the *salon*, comfortably dropping her posterior onto the moss-colored sofa (er, *canapé vert*). I wince, hoping the long-abused frame doesn't collapse under her 50 kilograms. The guards—formerly mere cockroaches, now properly trained and equipped—are bound to be no less concerned.

"Hello, Lily! How are you? Didn't expect to see you here today." I take my seat on the entertainment center, next to the television.

"Can you help me with another radio program? My audience really liked you." And there is her electric smile again. *I'm about to be asked for something significant, aren't I?*

"Sure, that would be fine. We could schedule something. What time…"

"Now!"

"*Now?*"

"Now!"

I nearly spill my tea

"You don't have your recorder with you. And what would we talk about?"

"No, we are going to the radio station." *Huh?* She catches my evident confusion. "This will be live!"

***

A less accommodating teacher might not indulge Lily and her sudden call to action, but my curiosity gets the best of me. Superficially disagreeable at times (although more as a student than a teacher), I am nevertheless helpful to a fault, at least when asked nicely. Thus, I close the Grand Château's gate, but the medium-density fiberboard of my door—an interior door by design, installed *on the exterior* of the apartment in a semi-monsoon climate—has swollen so thoroughly that the lock cannot latch.

If I had anything worth stealing, I would be worried.

We cross the bridge over *Celestial Lake*—the blue-green retention pond next to the foreign teachers' residential complex—and are at the library, which houses the campus radio station. Said *radio station* has neither a tower nor *radio* waves, nor is it a *station* in any recognizable sense. Instead, it is the on-room command center of the West Campus's closed-circuit public address system.

And we are not there.

Instead, Lily has dragged and overstretched cables out of the command center's window and planted several microphones on stands on a polymer card table. Around the table, there are four folding chairs—two occupied, one for Lily, and one (presumably) for me. *So we're having our interview al fresco?*

What follows is a two-minute introduction—*We welcome back our dear guest, Teacher Goble, and John Zhang and Layla Yang, our new special student guests, blah, blah, blah*—and a Chinese pop song about following one's dreams (or so I am told). Lily riffs off this—the power of passion, of doing what one believes she should, of free will and its connection to destiny, fates, the universe, and the greater good. I consider the possibility that I should have stayed at the Grand Château, doing whatever one does in his salon when not entertaining the highest of highborn guests—frying noodles and tossing brioche to the peasants. *(Or should the peasants be tossed noodles? Cultural considerations abound. And would the peonage even appreciate bowls of hot noodles being tossed from the balcony?)*

"Do you believe, Teacher Goble, you—who has come all the way from America, who traveled across the ocean to see—that we should follow our dreams?" *I'm seeing a theme here, am I not?*

This is one of Lily's patent persuasive tools—ask a question so disarmingly anodyne that answering it in the negative is nearly impossible, follow that with one incrementally less so, then another, then more after that. Eventually, she has you right where she wants you—agreeing to whatever she has in mind, and ignorant of how you got there.

"Well, I suppose," I tread lightly, "we should try," and I offer a monkish smile, my words softly spoken, nodding gently at the other guests. My lack of enthusiasm slows down Lily not at all.

Her voice rises, alarum and excursion loud, strains of patriotic fervor with such bombastic energy that I fear I may have stumbled into water beyond my depth. More dreams, more passion, more destiny! She turns to compatriots, who appear unfazed. *Am I making too much of this? Is this nothing more than student radio with Chinese characteristics?*

"And you, dear guests, dear beloved students, the future of our nation, do you believe we should follow our dreams, our hopes, our aspirations, or should we deny destiny, fate, and the energy of the Way?"

"Of course! Follow your dreams!" John answers without hesitation, his tone feather-light, buoyant, and eager to please. He might well be an acolyte of Lily. And yes, after less than a semester on campus, Lily has followers.

Years later, I will discover that Lily has a fan club—with a high school student as president, weekly chapter meetings in a second-floor private room of a local restaurant, and thereabouts of 20 members. *Why* they are fans—for what act, skill, or accomplishment they are fanning—will never be clear to me. *But no matter. I am showing my age: Celebrity is a circular thing, existing for its own sake.*

Lily is ahead of her time—a trendsetter. She is what a 2020s influencer might be if they were fully clothed, untainted by sex tapes, un(re)touched by makeup and surgical enhancements, and selling patriotic motivation and the importance of self-confidence instead of lip kits, shapewear, or tequila. (Not much like an influencer, I admit, but I find my comparisons where I can.)

Or maybe she is part of an older, more hallowed tradition.

"Yes, we should. We should follow our dreams. They are what make us human." Layla is less bombastic, more resolved, and her leaning into the microphone lends gravitas to counterbalance the Apostle John's freshly baptized energy.

Lily the proselytizer bounces around the table, excited—spreading the good news of freedom and hope—and stops passersby, asking leading questions about hopes and dreams that no sensible person could help but answer in the affirmative. I have seen street preachers in Los Angeles do the same, but with less grace. *Lily is all glory and redemption, not damnation and Revelation.* One student after the next is drawn into Lily's ministerial presence, each earnest reply a testimony in the service of the Word. I am half expecting her to pull a miniature dragon from her backpack and tame it with the power of positive thinking.

But such is not to be.

Instead, what follows is an invective/exhortation/sermon that would turn the sinning-est sinner to the Lord before he had time to let go of his harlot and drop his whiskey bottle.

Who would keep us from our destinies? Who would stand in the way of free will and divine intent? Who would dare to do this? The youth of China—the glory and pride of the Motherland—cannot, should not, will not be repressed. Lily tosses Buddha and Laozi into the mix. Chairman Mao (despite his hostility to both Buddhism and Daoism) follows shortly thereafter.

Voice climbing toward the heavens, her microphone held with a white-knuckled grip, Lily's sermon is reaching its divine crescendo.

"Who would do this? Would deny us our destinies?" she rallies. "Would you?" she asks, her microphone millimeters from Layla's face.

"No! I would not!"

"And you, Teacher Goble?"

"Oh," I wait a beat, everything falls into place, and I realize I am being asked to provide material support in Layla's spiritual war. One—probably several—administrators are bound to be annoyed. *Well, so long as they are in a different department...* "I would certainly hope not!"

John affirms the sentiment.

"Why then would the Department of Business not allow a promising young student—a dedicated student, a determined student who wants to make her country better, to change majors?" *Modest, aren't we, Lily.* "Why would they stand in the way of those who are so very eager to help our nation share her culture and 5,000 years of glorious history with the world, with foreign friends such as Dear Teacher Goble? Why would they do this?" She inhales, "That is the question I leave you with tonight, beloved listeners. That is the question I have for *you!*" She twists her face into a smile so broad I nearly hop out of my seat. "Goodbye, beloved listeners. Until tomorrow!"

And cut to music!

Someone in the control room must have found the presentation interesting—the latter half had been broadcast over every loudspeaker on campus. I offer my best golf clap. Lily's acolytes are less reserved.

"Teacher, let's get you back home!" And so it goes; I am back at the Château in minutes, with the acolytes being left to put away the table and gear.

Right before I close the door, Lily turns back to me in the hallway, dropping her stage smile. "Thanks again, Dear Teacher Goble," and despite her little wink, I think she means.

Was I part of a coup?

***

Two days later, Lily appears in my class, apparently now a student in the English department.

None of my Chinese colleagues have said a word to me about Lily and her theatrics. In truth, they likely do not care about my participation. *You are a White person. You have no face*—when one of my Chinese friends tells me this, I am uncertain whether I should be offended.

I should not. Such is a statement of fact, nothing more.

Face (miànzi) has no precise Western equivalent. With elements of pride, dignity, importance, and self-perception, it lacks the firm Western distinction between the public and private selves. The easiest way to imagine it is something akin to a mixture of reputation (both personal and professional) and self-regard. I do not have this. I *cannot* have this—*my self* is not one, but many distinct pieces, each compartmentalized and semi-autonomous. Such is the end product of *being the product* of an individualistic society. Collectivistic thinking can never be wholly understood from the outside. Even if I were to merge my public and private selves, the collective would never acknowledge as much and recognize me as being part of it. Thus, *no face*.

This—being a faceless outsider—has its advantages.

Foremost is that I can operate with the scantest of social graces, skirting the limits of proper decorum without running past them. This is not to suggest that I am *rude*. I remain formally polite, but no one—*no one*—expects me to take a hint. I can ramble on and about as I wish, popping in and out of many places and a great many more conversations without causing ill will, so long as I do so with a smile and an expression of innocent curiosity. In Japan and South Korea— nations in which the concept of face is no less paramount than in China—foreigners are sometimes hired (or so I have been told) for exactly this reason: They are useful fools, yodeling out what the locals would never dare (despite someone needing to say it), skipping over protocols, and waltzing away with the lightest of social repercussions.

I have no way of ascertaining whether Lily considered as much, or knew the extent of my befuddled foreign superpowers, but protect me, those powers did nonetheless.

***

Crack!

"Ow!"

Crack!

"Ow!"

Crack!

Stop. *Huff! Ring! Ring! Mumble, mumble.*

Wait! Is someone taking a call?

How I ended up in here—in this dentist's chair at the city's *most affordable* hospital—waiting for the doctor to finish his phone call as his assistant holds my jaw open, with little tooth fragments covering both of us, is worthy of some explanation.

***

Of all the powers *Le Baron Brant de Goblé, Grand Déconcerté de l'Empire du Milieu* (meaning *me*, the *Grandly Confused One of the Middle Kingdom*), possesses, dental resilience is not amongst them. This unpleasant realization dawns on me when a sharp pain sets off slow-wave oscillations in my jaw, rattling their way into my head and spine, and prompting noble curses from me sufficient to alarm the insect guards and rattle them from their posts.

I ignore this, despite the pain gradually ratcheting up, and carry on with my days. Ambling about from campus to campus, I learn which restaurants offer passable meals—fried cabbage and rice being a newfound favorite—and which offer (heavily discounted) food poisoning. This occupies whatever portion of my time and attention is not consumed by teaching. The little aches, the rumbling of one's stomach, the ear that itches at random, the sore feet—the body is constantly complaining, and the complaints are far more likely to be noise than signal. For every horror story one hears of someone who ignored a deadly serious problem, there are thousands more—usually untold—of a problem that went away on its own.

But such is not to be the case for me.

Thus, after weeks of wincing my way through one bite after bite of Hunanese spiciness, I (gingerly) bite the bullet, pull out my counterfeit TCL dumbphone, and call Lawrence.

"Hello!" I can hear the gnawing of betel nut husks and Lawrence taking a puff of his cigarette. The sun may have risen above the horizon mere minutes ago, but Lawrence is a man of consistency.

"Lawrence, one of my teeth is," I am struggling to avoid any needlessly dramatic terminology—despite the aching, "less than optimal."

"Huh?!" *gnaw, gnaw, slurp!* (another Red Bull, presumably), "Do you need to go to a dentist?"

I turn the matter around in my head. The matter of money comes to mind, and with my salary being the equivalent of a hair less than 600 dollars a month, I am unhesitatingly willing to *Cast Away* my tooth before I allow a dentist to yank more than 200 yuan—about 30 dollars—from my pocket. Surely someone in China sells ice skates (or *an ice skate*—I need but one).

"How much will it cost?"

"Don't know, but we can see."

***

The day of my appointment, Lawrence arrives at the campus gate. He is driving a tiny, gray Toyota of a model I have never seen before.

"Nice car, Lawrence." I buckle in. At all of 173 cm and 55 kg (or 5'8" and 120 pounds, if you prefer), I can fit in the seat, snugly. I understand why this car is not sold in the United States—the stick shift would end up as a colon probe for a not inconsiderable percentage of my fellow compatriots, and given the stick's shape, I doubt they would appreciate this as part of the performance package.

"So, Lawrence, where are we going?"

"People's Hospital Number 2."

This is a mistake of the greenest of green hands—not seeking advice, suggestions, or recommendations before choosing a hospital, and not taking into account that Lawrence, for all his relaxed good-naturedness, is bound to select whatever institution is closest.

The hospital has a spotless exterior, red calligraphic signage, dark-cyan windows with a low-e coating that remind me of a calm sea, stone-tile walls, and an all but empty parking lot. It looks modern enough in the high-ceilinged, sharp-echoed way that modern Chinese constructions often do. And it is nearly empty, which I take as a good sign of fast service to come.

And fast it is! Ushered up a staircase and into the dentist's office, I am greeted by the good doctor himself—an older man with a pate obscured by a scattering of thin hairs doing their heroic best to shield it from the sun and a gut tucked behind a smock with straining buttons. *Chinese men go bald? Really?* A much younger man, rail-thin, silent, in a white smock of his own (*the assistant?*), stands to the side.

In the matter of a minute, I am poked, scraped, and told one of my wisdom teeth must be removed *today* and that payment can be arranged at the counter (for a low, low price to boot!).

Hustle down two flights of stairs, forfeit a token sum, collect a receipt, hustle up again—and I plop back down in the reclining chair for what I am unreasonably confident will be a process of no more than 15 or 20 minutes.

The dental assistant, having donned gloves, holds my jaw open. The dentist starts mumbling in a dialect, seemingly at me. (I may not speak much Mandarin, but I can tell *this* is not *that*.)

"Lawrence," I pause, working my jaw free of the assistant's grip, "what is he saying?"

"Oh!" *slurp*, "they are going to give you an injection."

My catalog of phobias is extensive—heights (*I'm dizzy already*), open spaces (*drones, drones everywhere!*), and bulls (*why the anger? I didn't eat your family.*)—but needles are not amongst them. So, the pressure on my gums and the disconcerting numbness propagating through the bones of my *no-face face* bothers me not at all.

Then, as the assistant is about the place the thin paper drape over my face, I catch the glint of light off a hammer.

This intrigues me, but in my endless optimism, I am nearly ready to dismiss it as being somehow, someway, unrelated to my mouth. *Why in heaven's name would he need a hammer?*

And then, lifting the drape up for a moment, I see the awl.

In truth, the tools the dentist has in his hands—an osteotome and a surgical mallet—are better suited to the joyless task before us and *supposedly* better quality than what one is likely to find in the average garage (unless one has the budget for *Snap-on*, but honestly, my jaw isn't worthy of that quality of equipment). One hopes they are somewhat cleaner.

"Hul-woe, Lawlence ..." I am struggling to speak; my tongue is tingly-numb. "Why the hammer?"

"They are going to remove your tooth." Lawrence's voice is distant, echoing off the tiles. *How far away is he standing?*

The assistant forces open my jaw as far as he can.

"Ow!"

"Maybe you should not move too much." At this point, Lawrence sounds as though he may well be calling out from behind a blast wall. *What are they planning? Does it involve drilling and shaped charges?* I am about to be amused by this idea—of having a tooth removed according to the Wile E. Coyote School of Dentistry protocol. *Pity how the foreigner lost his head, though, face or no-face.*

Then ...

Crack!

"Ow!"

Crack!

"Ow!"

My *owwws!* are less a matter of pain than they are anxiety. My jaw is numb (more or less), but hammer blows are jarring, more so because they are landing inches away from my orbital sockets.

Stop. I hear the dentist clank down his hammer on the table. He shuffles around tools. There are pliers in my mouth. He tugs, mumbles, tugs again. Something comes loose, but I can't tell if it is giving way or being wiggled unproductively. He puts down the pliers.

Was that it? That wasn't so ...

Crack!

"Ow!"

The tempo of the blows is slower—the dentist must be taking larger swings. Every half-dozen minutes, he stops, mutters, gives the three of us—me, him, and the assistant trying to keep my head from getting *Oldboy-ed*—a break. What *isn't* breaking is the tooth, which is so deeply embedded in my jaw that a proper steel-driving man would have no better luck.

I can sympathize with the dentist's frustration. He is in an unenviable position. But mine is not much better. With every strike, the masseter, temporalis, and medial pterygoid—all the muscles that allow me to prattle through my days and afford the luxury of name-brand (and presumably non-recycled) cooking oil—are being stretched so far that my jaw dropping to the floor might well become more than an expression.

I am a tad less sympathetic to the phone calls.

Crack! Crack! Crack! (Pause, big swing. I inhale, brace myself.)

Ring! Ring!

The hammer drops (on the table, not my head).

"*Wèi?*"

And that—*hello*—is about as much of the dentist's conversation as I can understand. The assistant relaxes his grip.

"Lawr-enz... wa... iz... z. ... den-ist... doin?"

"Oh," *chew, chew, and other betel nut noises,* "he is talking to his wife."

"Oh! Ooh-kay!"

Talking might be too generous a term; it sounds as though the healthcare provider is planning to *provide* his wife with proper end-of-life (or *life-ending*) care, possibly by way of defenestration, *and soon*, likely against her wishes. But herein lies a problem with the many dialects of Chinese—despite Chinese being a tonal language, one cannot very well gauge mood from the speaker's pitch or amplitude. The happy couple might well be discussing what to have for dinner, their child's grades, or the dentist exceeding his monthly mallet budget. Perhaps the wife exceeded hers. I am left to guess.

After three more injections, an additional 45 minutes of hammering, and two more phone calls, we are done. This hour has taken a week. The drape is removed from my face, my glasses are returned to me, and I stand up on pectin legs. The doctor hands me two extra-strength acetaminophen, and I shake his and his assistant's hands and am given a box of antibiotics. The men appear no less drained than I am.

Lawrence looks up from his phone. He stops chewing; the clanking of the hammer, if not the flying remains of my tooth, had perforated, however finely, his bubble of monk/camel imperturbability. He is a shade paler than when we started.

"You okay?"

"Ne-er been bett-ur." *Huh?* My tongue is still stubbornly immobile, if not outright dead. *That'll probably clear up by morning.*

***

Sleeping for more than minutes at a time proves impossible—the pain, not bad for several hours after the procedure, sawtooth waves through my jaw with all the delicacy of a lightning bolt from midnight to the morning reveille—a patriotic song blaring through the campus's loudspeakers at half past six. I would stay at home, but the Chinese are parsimonious with sick days, and I prefer not to waste one on something as trivial as what I fear (incorrectly) is a broken jaw.

I shower, scour, and dress, then wave farewell to the loyal guards of the Château, wishing them an uneventful shift, before taking the brief shuttle ride to the East Campus. I am weak, tired, and still wired, but presumably in good enough condition for government work, which, fortuitously, is precisely what I am paid to do.

It isn't until I have climbed seven flights of stairs, situated myself behind the desk, chalk in hand, and try to speak that I encounter the problem *du jour*.

"Hey, eh-we-one, to-hay we are goin'" I bite my tongue. *Ow!* I certainly felt that. *So what's the problem?*

"Hel-woe, eh-we-one," and I realize my jaw won't open more than fractions of an inch. I take a moment to massage the muscles.

I try again.

"Hel-woe..." *Nope!* So, fearing I might inadvertently propagate bad pronunciation on my vulnerable charges, I write *A little problem. Read books! I will return!* on the chalkboard and excuse myself, leaving my students but slightly less bewildered than was Captain Benteen upon receiving Colonel Custer's last message.

Away from the students' curious eyes, I take stock of the situation. My tongue is still partially numb from the procedure yesterday, but its function is unimpaired. My larynx, despite a low-grade sore throat, is operational. So I have two of three essential speech organs—and that should count for something.

The problem is the jaw itself—forcing it open doesn't work. Massaging and pressure make no difference. Mostly closed, it is determined to stay.

Hmm! There has to be something—some way to adapt. Ah!

WWAVD? What would a ventriloquist do?

There is a trick to enunciating without fully opening one's mouth: The tongue is operated normally, pressing against the teeth and palate as it is wont to do. As for the larynx, a professional would subdue its movement for the best effect, but that is beyond the scope of my autodidactic crash course. What really demands attention is the jaw itself, the movements of which must be adjusted *relative to one another*—outsized movements become small ones, and small ones become barely perceptible. Keep the ratios the same, and...

I can speak!

My pronunciation isn't terrible—my *r*'s and *l*'s are indistinguishable, but I am firmly back in the realm of intelligibility. The most significant issue is a lack of volume, which I anticipate will not be catastrophic given my students' careful manners and reservoir of goodwill.

***

After a morning of acting as my own puppet (minus any challenging hand or arm insertions), I am, if not confident in my abilities to persevere, considerably *less unconfident* than I was at sunrise.

Returning to the Château, I discover that nothing is amiss save my head. It, not without its problems on the best of days, is throbbing with such energetic pulsing consistency that I am about to ask my faithful guards to wheel out their insect-sized guillotine and hack away. Presumably, they would start at my crown and work their way to my neck. (I am nothing if not patient for relief.) I know the real problem is my jaw and the tendons around it, but this does little to ease the referred pain. I massage my temples for a moment. The day is Friday, and the thought of sitting at home with nothing other than my tiny sentinels and my super-sized misery is not something I relish. I accept that I will be neither sleeping nor eating for days, and I am doubtful of my ability to drink anything without the aid of a straw.

So what to do?

My last class of the day had been an enthusiastic one, so much so that I was intrigued by the fuss. I initially attributed this to the upcoming weekend, but (and I say this with magic crystals and essential oils in hand) the *vibe was something different*. Being nosy, I asked what, if anything, was happening.

"We are going on a field trip to Fenghuang!" a girl—smiling, small, and with a name that I struggle to recall—chirps.

"*Feng*, where?" I say it loud enough for the front of the class to hear me.

"Fenghuang! It is an old and beautiful city," another student pipes in. *Titter, titter*, and a short discussion ensues in Mandarin. Several students nod—a consensus has been reached. "Would you like to come, Teacher?"

"Oh! How kind," I take a moment, not positive of what to make of the offer, "maybe sometime…"

And here is another little cultural lesson: As an American, I reflexively regard any such offers as symbolic, in the same vein as asking *How are you?* No one really cares how you are, and God help us if you give an honest answer. But in China, an offer to go on a trip or a dinner invitation—these are made in sincerity more often than not, hence:

"Okay, but you have an hour to decide. We are leaving soon." And the student hands me a slip of paper with her phone number on it.

I take in the bare walls of the Château, and the throbbing intensifies. *What to do? Should I stay here?* Pain is the worst sort of company, especially when you have no other. But travel will exhaust me. *What to do? What to do?* I exhale, irritated at my indecision. *Ugh, anything has to be better than sitting at home!* So I pull out my candy bar TCL and dial the number.

"*Wei?*"

"Hello! This is Teacher Goble. I was curious if you are still interested in having me on the trip."

"Yes! Yes! But you must hurry. We are going to the train station soon."

"Where are..."

"It is okay," *laugh*, "someone will come and get you. Be ready!" *Click!*

The *someone will come and get you* is a kind touch—at this point, my complete lack of a sense of direction has earned me a curious acclaim. No one, Lawrence included, asks me to find anything new. They either pop in unannounced or message me to ask me to meet them at a familiar landmark.

As I am putting the second set of socks, the first pair of underwear, and a box of antibiotics in my drab surplus PLA messenger bag that I pulled from my closet—*knock, knock! Knock, knock!*

"Teacher Goble?" *Knock, knock! Knock, knock!* "Teacher Goble!"

I get to the door as speedily as I can. Yanking it free of the frame takes effort, and my fatigue makes the undertaking feel as though I were Samson pulling down the temple of Dagon.

"Hel..."

"We must hurry, Teacher!"

And so we—me and one of the class's two male students, who graciously offers to carry my half-pound of luggage—are on our way to the bus stop in front of the gate in under a minute.

***

At the train station, I mention to a student that I don't have a ticket, but I am assured I needn't worry. And this is correct. Rather than each of us going through the turnstiles, we form a throng, with one of the students—the leader of the gang, I suppose—waving a fistful of paper at the ticket collector, while the others chatter energetically. The collector nods in my direction, and the students yell *Teacher!* in English in response. The man knows he's outnumbered and lets us through.

This seems chaotic, but it works. In a culture as high-context as China's, people know how it—whatever it is—works implicitly, in social interactions, if nothing else. Some official proclamations are to be taken seriously; others demand such but rarely. Others still can be safely ignored altogether. This is also true of officials, institutions, deadlines, and nearly everything else. The Chinese are experts at reading between the lines, which both impresses and exasperates me, depending on the day and circumstances.

Hence, whatever the students arranged regarding my fare.

On a more scrupulous day, I might have objected to my students' tactics and insisted on buying a ticket in the ordinary fashion—such is the strength of ancestral German impulse to follow the rules. But between the (incompletely removed) tooth, the sleepless night, and my ever-tightening jaw, I let the giggling gaggle guide me onto the train, trusting that I have not committed some grave transgression.

I like trains—a statement I imagine suggests I am either on the autism spectrum, hipsterishly old-fashioned, or some combination thereof. But it's true.

The hustle and hurry as people board and alight at each stop. The locomotive pulling away, power rising—a gently awakening giant. The *clack-clack* of old fishplated tracks when the machine is on the move, and the primly uniformed snack seller's singsong call as she pushes her overstuffed cart down the narrow aisle. This is motion. This is progress.

To be on a train is to be *going somewhere* with the force of future-past industry and tons of momentum.

And it's better than the buses.

If my journey with Ethan to Jiawei was exciting in a BASE-jumping sort of way, the trip from the campus to the train station was the kind of traumatizing that comes from being ejected from an F-16 into a hurricane. The driver, a dainty woman who couldn't have weighed more than 45 kilograms, took the command to *drive it like you stole it* so seriously that I was half expecting the police to be in hot pursuit. I *suspect* she understood gears and the transmission, if only to the extent she knew she would never actually have to downshift from fifth so long as she worked the clutch hard with pure rock fury. And if she barked orders loudly enough at the passengers, they would take the hint and jump off at their designated stop (if not sooner).

This might have been overcompensation on her part—a jumbo-sized Napoleon complex stuffed into a takeaway-sized frame and armed with a multi-ton vehicle.

Tenderness to our deficiencies can make us irrational.

But I might not be giving this slight creature enough credit, and her superego could well have constructed a methodical madness—with every pedestrian she flattens, said driver incrementally lowers the average height of the city, thus making herself *comparatively* taller—such is the joy of percentiles.

The train itself is quaint, if too warm from the crush of bodies and the forever humid air of Hunan. Pulled by a diesel locomotive and featuring carriages in hunter and cream livery with hard seats, it is hardly more modern than one I recall from *The Legend of Drunken Master*. This is the second occasion I have had to be on a Chinese train—the first being a redeye trip to Changsha with Lawrence for a medical examination, in which the quiet *clack-clack*, however rhythmic and calming it might have been, kept me awake—excited and attentive to every sound and flicker of passing light. Lawrence, not knowing me well at the time and preoccupied with official tasks, said no more than necessary, leaving me to my own thoughts.

Now, I am surrounded by cheerful chatter.

The train slows to a stop at a tiny single-platform station, a voice zap-cracks over the intercom, and we disembark on the outskirts of Fenghuang. Years later, there will be a better, faster train to the place and a sleek train station with gracefully curved eaves and a futuristic interior.

But for now, there is the old station, and from there, we—thereabouts of 30 of us—cram into two minibuses, and we are on our way. We bounce along the road, but slowly, with all in good spirits—a welcome change from the ride of terror across Huaihua.

The countryside rolling by us is idyllic, with rice paddies and brick kilns scattered over rolling verdant expanses. Flowers dotting the fields blur into color, to some extent distracting me from my jaw.

We approach the tourist trap/ancient city/peanut-candy Mecca of central Hunan, its brown stone walls growing taller. The minibuses pull to a smooth stop, and we are in front of *another* gate. This one, tall and formidable, is crowned with a two-tiered pavilion with a traditional tile roof and steeply upturned eaves. The red lanterns festooning the pavilion and the banners hanging down the gate's thick walls contrast with the mass of the thing—a twinkle in the eye of a hulking ox.

We're through that in a minute, and I am at a loss.

Fenghuang is a city on a river, with old wooden buildings on stilts looming over the meandering water, even older stone buildings behind them, lush hills in the distance, and lanterns—more lanterns—everywhere. I am half expecting to see men with queues flying above the tourists, their robes fluttering loudly as they kick. But no luck.

Later, I will mention to a Chinese friend that I was disappointed, if but weakly, that I had yet to see so much as a single kung fu fight in all my months in China, much less an acrobatic one.

A dear woman with a mop haircut and bangs that remind me of a puppy's ears, she'll put down her mug of dancing fairy tea and pretends surprise, briefly. Her nearly irrepressible smile—one that will survive the misfortune of not one, but two dates with me—unaltered, she'll apologize mock-seriously, swearing she will do her best to arrange something.

Anyway. Fenghuang is *different* from the *modernish* campus, *different* from chaotic Huaihua, *different* from anywhere I have seen outside of a movie. I stand for a minute, disoriented, taking in the place, a pleasant surrealness enveloping me, as though there had been a mighty flash powder *pop!* and I had awoken in the middle of a postcard.

A student—one of the best in class, reserved and with a poise that belies her youth—catches the smile spreading across my swollen face.

"Teacher, do you like the city?" Her eyes smile. She knows the answer.

"I do," but before I can say more, I swoon a bit. My day without water is starting to enervate me.

"Are you okay, Teacher?"

"A little dizzy. It's nothing."

"You're sure?" She's skeptical.

I pause. *Exactly how much of a pain should I be? How much can one reasonably complain?*

"Something to drink might help," I say with considerable effort, but the words come out weak, and this little utterance adds to my dizziness.

And the student takes me by the arm, gently, as though I were a gentleman of 85.

***

At the little table, where we settle in for a bottle of sweet red tea, I finally get a glance of myself in the river flowing by us. *Ugh!* Both plain-faced and (apparently) no-faced, I avoid mirrors most mornings. Shaving by touch, I regard any efforts not resulting in decapitation as being good enough, and I brush my teeth in the shower. So I am horrified/amused to see that my jaw and cheeks had swollen to chipmunk proportions.

"I look terrible!"

Snort!

That's the other student sitting across from me. This one, the reserved one's friend, is more effusive by far, and she's been a pleasant companion for minutes. But it's her outfit that I can't help but notice. Her vest, which would be at home on any dude ranch, and a leather cowboy hat she picked up at a nearby stall are distinctive enough, but it's the white shirt, dappled in black in a decidedly bovine pattern, that ties it all together. There's a common thread here. And I consider the possibility that the shirt was chosen due to a subtle cross-cultural misunderstanding, with the student believing that *cowgirls* need to camouflage themselves so the cattle are not disturbed.

Either way, I wait to see if she has anything to add to her nasal interjection.

"It's not that bad, Teacher. I had my teeth hammered, too!"

"You mean this is normal?" I point to my face.

"Yep!"

"Oh? I thought they were torturing me because I'm a capitalist."

"Huh?" offers the reserved one. *Well, that joke was a dud.*

We slowly finish our drinks and wander around the city, my students correcting me when I go too far off course. Others redirect me if I escape the snare and wander farther still.

This is a peculiar feeling for me—to be *minded*, for someone to notice if I disappear, to have someone come looking. For all my thoughts bouncing and scattering, their shooting straight to the distant horizon, they never landed here—somewhere I would be *known*. Waves and ghosts are not much different—they pass through walls, with little trace but faint energy. Nor had I, being a constellation of ghosts and the spirit of confusion, left much more than an ectoplasm of academic transcripts and administrative recordings in scattered databases. But Hunan is a different place.

Here I am plainly visible.

The day passes, evening sets in, and the air grows clammy-cool. The city lights up—with Hongqiao Bridge, a multistoried covered structure resting atop stone arches, lit up in orange, green, and red. The river glows with shimmering, fluorescent reflections. Fenghuang, like its namesake, *the Fenghuang*, is a composite. Roughly translated as *Chinese Phoenix*, the Fenghuang shares naught with its Western counterpart but wings. Yet despite not having been reborn from the ashes, the Fenghuang is an ambitious, if perplexing, construction of myth.

Polychromatic and feminine, the Fenghuang is said to have the head of a golden pheasant, the body of a mandarin duck, the tail of a peacock, the legs of a crane, the mouth of a parrot, and the wings of a swallow. (And that is the more airworthy iteration—with the older myths saying it is equal parts bird, snake, tortoise, stag, and fish.) And in this way, it suits its namesake city well—part ethnic minority, part Han; part museum, part tourist attraction; part old, part new, and part new pretending to be old. The mix is a mystifying one for the Western mind, at least mine, which draws on clean lines between mental spaces and purposes—that sorts music by the strict rules of genre, divides the person and persona cleanly (hence no face), and distinguishes the counterfeit from the authentic. Yet standing in Fenghuang, in the heart of the phoenix's dominion, I can appreciate the flow of hybridity.

We—the two students and I—have picked up snacks as we've gone along. Other students walk with us more often than not, but less consistently, with these two seeming to have accepted responsibility for keeping me—the *Grandly Confused One*—from wandering into the water, being dragged away by trinket sellers, or falling head-first into a boat and disappearing into the mist. As for the snacks, the little treats are both tantalizingly close and unreachably far away.

First, there is *jiāngtáng*, a rock-hard candy made from sugar mixed with Hunan ginger, then pulled, folded, and pulled again until it forms ropey strands. *Smells great! Can't eat it, but smells great!* Then there is *huāshēngbǐng*—roasted peanuts and caramelized sugar, mixed into a paste, and pounded with oversized mallets until cakey, crumbly, and airy. *(I can't eat that either! And my God, these people love their hammers!)*

When (or *if!*) my jaw recovers, I'll enjoy these. Until then, into my bag they go.

Eventually, we find a restaurant with passable prices and rough wooden benches. At my minders' suggestion, I settle on a plate of *mápó dòufu*—which can be translated as either "Pockmarked Grandma's Tofu" or "Grandma's Numbing Tofu," and which consists of bite-sized pieces of soft tofu fried in oil, chili, and Sichuan peppercorns. It's a good fit, metaphorically and literally—I could use a good numbing, my no-face/face, if not pockmarked, is far from its middling best, and the tofu cubes are small and soft enough to slip between my teeth.

I can slide grains of rice in as well, slowly—and with each bite, I am feeling more myself—weak, but not dead.

After dinner, the class assembles at a designated point near a bridge and returns to the hotel—an old building made of thin gray bricks and with a sliding wooden door. Weak or not, I notice the *shíjǐn chuāng* windows—a traditional Chinese style, defined by glass divided into irregular squares and rectangles by complex wooden latticework, and more common in prosperous northern homes. They, like me, are out of place.

My students are packed five or ten to a room, but I have the good fortune of having one of my own—a cold space with a hard bed and a rough blanket. The building's age *partially* explains its lack of heat. The rest of the explanation is one of geography. South of the Huai River—the traditional boundary between northern and southern China—the weather was deemed sufficiently/tolerably warm year-round by the powers that be for indoor heating to be a waste of energy. There are other differences between the regions, ranging from dietary preferences to sociability and drinking culture—but this one, the matter of indoor heating, is one of the most pertinent to a half-frozen, hammer-bruised foreigner.

Northern-style windows, Spartan southern accommodations.

I pull my antibiotics from my messenger bag, pop two of them, as per the doctor's orders, wrap myself in the cold blanket, and immediately fall asleep, sitting upright, my head hanging down to keep my jaw from throbbing more severely than it must.

***

I wake up to energetic rapping on my door—*knock, knock, knock!*

Was that a woodpecker?

"Teacher! Teacher!" *Knock! Knock! Knock!* "We must go! Are you ready?"

No, but I don't answer as much. Instead, I stand up, shuffle to the bathroom, messenger bag in hand, and spend three minutes trying to make myself presentable. I am not as tired as I thought I would be, and my head, while still aching, seems to be functioning, well enough to guide me through my ablutions and get me out the door.

I'm in the lobby in another minute and checked out of the inn after another two. And we are all back in the narrow alley, ready for another day of exploring in the overcast light of a still-chill morning.

After a bottle of juice (sipped through a straw), I am energetic enough to climb the *Southern Great Wall*. Wall—singular—is a misnomer. There are numerous Southern Great Walls scattered throughout lower China (rather than a continuous wall, as exists in the north). And the longest of them, constructed of substantial red stone, is in Fenghuang. About three meters tall and two meters thick, the Fenghuang Wall is sufficient to keep out invaders who have yet to invent the ladder, which is not to say I want to fall off it. I shakily make my way up the steps, my two guiding students close behind, and take in the view.

The Wall is a reconstruction, not so much an incremental Ship-of-Theseus replacement as an outright rebuild from memory and imagination after the original was dismantled for its materials. Still, the reconstruction is impressive. And at the top, there are industrious women, offering rayon costumes, elaborately embroidered, for rent. For a trivial number of yuan, anyone can be a high-ranking mandarin for a moment, *including me*. So, to the tremendous amusement of the costume renters, fellow tourists, and guiding students alike, I don yellow robes, gently place a large, ornate red hat on my head, and pick up a delicate Qing-style fan.

A couple of photos with my point-and-shoot digital Canon (which I extract from my bag with some difficulty, trying to avoid dumping my underwear on the ground in the process), and memories are made. We return the costume, descend the Wall, and take more photos along the way. Later, I dress up as a Miao (one of the dominant non-Han minorities in the region) and pretend to play a flute, the river babbling in front of me.

Guo—a quiet, often-smiling young man invited by his student-friend—takes the trip's final photo. The class assembles in front of the city's symbolic center—a bronze Fenghuang statue in the middle of a dry fountain, old in design, modern in construction. The students arrange themselves into three rows: some standing on the pavement, others on the red stone rim of the fountain, and those in the front kneeling. About half of them make the V-sign with their hands. An overcast sky and the traditional wooden buildings behind us, I'm near the middle, wearing a borrowed cowboy hat. Everyone is young and seemingly happy.

This memory will stay with me for years.

I'll remember the pain in my jaw, the dizziness, and the still-persistent weakness in my legs, arms, neck, and everywhere else. And I'll know that had I not ignored those, had I stayed home and indulged my misery with the zap-waves of locked tendons and my traumatized gums and the guards of the Château for company, I would have missed this day. I'll look to it when I feel inclined to quit, the smiling faces, mine included, gently rebuking me.

Not long after, we depart—back on minibuses, back on a train, back on a city bus-of-terror (*sponsored by Red Bull, presumably*), and then back to campus. The sun breaks through the clouds on the journey's last leg, and the warmth through the window loosens my jaw by a millimeter— something for which I am grateful.

From the gate, I'm shepherded the full few hundred meters by Guo and a student, lest I get lost on a journey over familiar terrain. The Château's gate is completely swollen into the frame—more so than when I left—making it a three-man job to open. But we overcome! The guards scatter—discipline and morale must have decayed in my absence. I am back home, and with the bare minimum of mental presence, I ask Guo to copy some photos from his camera to my computer.

I'm glad I did.

***

As little rest as there may be for the wicked, there is even less for me, so back to work I go on a drizzly Monday. And in one of my classes is Lily. She's perky (as expected) and monopolizing the conversation, oblivious to her glaring peers, who, I have been told in private, find her eager-beaver interjections throughout class less a sign of dedication than abrasive overconfidence.

"But Teacher Goble," Lily smiles, all innocence and light.

"Yes, Lily?"

"I am confused about the speech. How long do we have to prepare?"

"This is an extemporaneous speech, so you look at the slip you pulled from the hat and spend five minutes preparing to speak. Take notes, if you please. Or not!" I smile as much as my still hammer-beaten face will allow.

"But I don't know when people should be fed to lions," a (usually) untalkative student pipes up from the back.

I give the wheels in my head a moment to start turning, trying to consider her comment with appropriate cultural sensitivity. *China never had lions, did it? No wonder she's at a loss.*

"Would it help if you substituted tigers?"

"Not really."

"Oh well, do the best you can," I rub my temples, gently, trying to loosen my slowly ratcheting temporalis muscles—a fan-shaped clutch of fibers growing tighter with each pulse of my painful (possibly pointless) pedantry.

Lily's eyes narrow. She knows something is off.

***

I dismiss class, and the students nearly bounce out of their chairs—time for lunch! The last session of every morning bounds out of the room as though their hair, feet, and rear ends have been doused in naphtha and set on fire. I find this curious for a while—the canteen's offerings, while fine, are unremarkable. *How excited can one get about a bowl of fried cabbage?* The answer, of course, is *very much so* if one has not eaten since the night before, as is the case more often than not. Given the ungodly early hour at which students are roused from their beds by reveille and made to drag themselves to my inedible (or at best *stringy*) presence, hunger is unavoidable.

Thus, I have taken to bringing candy with me from time to time, which I purchase in bulk from the campus store. The type I buy the most, White Rabbit—a soft, chewy candy that resembles a vanilla Tootsie Roll—is both popular with students and so inexpensive that it's nearly free. Thus, the sight of me trundling through the morning frost in my greatcoat, bags of candy in hand, has become one of welcome amusement. And the knowledge that any day may be Candy Day improves attendance to boot.

Lily, observing that I might well end up inflicting dental damage equal to my own on entire department sections, is less impressed. And she has a point—misery loves company, which might well explain why she is standing before me after her classmates have departed.

"Lily, is everything okay?"

"You sounded rather uncomfortable today, Teacher." And she's right: my jaw is still tight enough that speaking is difficult, and it's getting progressively worse throughout the day.

"A little pain, nothing fatal... probably."

"Why don't you go to the hospital?"

I shudder, determined to avoid Dr. Thor and his tender mercies until Ragnarök, if not until long after.

"That's where the problem started."

After some back and forth, Lily convinces me that *something* should be done, so I agree to return to People's Hospital Number 2, this time with Lily accompanying me and assuring me that no part of me will be hammered, scraped, cudgeled, or chopped. The walk is a speedy one over flat topography, but it's long enough to catch up. *Yes, the job is fine. Yes, I am making progress on my master's degree. Yes, I should finish it next year. And how about you? Are you glad you transferred to the English department?*

Yep! All is well. Now, I can learn the English language to help my fellow patriots compete more effectively in the global economy, spread Chinese culture, and promote thinking with Chinese characteristics...

Lily carries on, each of her motives more patriotic than the last, undisturbed by the pall of dampness insinuating its way through our clothes, and with so much bombast that part of me is waiting for her to break into a rendition of "The East Is Red" while flipping a Type 79 rifle in the air with drill-team precision.

I don't doubt that Lily is patriotic, but I've noticed that her passion for the motherland grows more clamorous immediately before she asks a favor. *Hence...*

"So, Lily, thanks for the help, but," I think, trying to keep my phrasing diplomatic, "can I do anything for you?"

"No, Dear Teacher! Why would you say that?" Lily feigns offense. *Oh, the poor girl!* "I want nothing more than to assist *my elder*!" There's a mischievous lilt on *my elder*.

"Sorry!"

"But since you mention it, Dear Teacher," *Again, with the Dear Teacher, hmm.* "Perhaps you can help my dear students with…" she stops. "We can talk about it later."

***

The sight of the hospital makes me squirm, and I very nearly turn back, with Lily's coaxing being all that keeps me marching forward into the stone-cool lobby. She talks to the nurse at reception for a minute, and I am directed up the stairs, past the chamber of hammer horrors—*whew!*—and to an icy white room with an examination table. I lie down, remove my glasses as per instructions, and a pad is placed on my jaw. The nurse turns a knob on the control unit to which the pad is wired, and my jaw slowly warms.

"What is this, Lily? What are they doing?" The setup seems elaborate for a heating pad.

She asks the nurse. Lily is as puzzled as I am for a moment.

"It is," she stops, asking another question, "short radio therapy?… Something about radios."

I slide my glasses back on and squint at the control unit—*27.12 MHz?* And I do some mental math. *That's the 11-meter band—shortwave.* (More precisely, it's the U.S. CB band—more *10-4, good buddy*, less Voice of Russia—but close enough.)

This is most dialed in of coincidences—me (electro)magnetically drawn here, to have said waves pulsing through my jaw, unknotting my yammer muscles. But apparitions and energies pull us to-and-fro in the most curious of ways, amusing themselves as we search for patterns.

I shiver under my coat. The nurse notices and hands me a blanket. More comfortable, the pain easing, I nod off under the comfort of a familiar frequency.

***

On the way back to the East Campus—where I will take the shuttle to the *other campus*—I am waiting for Lily's pitch. The schlepping me to the hospital took time, staying there with me took longer, and walking me back requires more effort still—this much work cannot be for naught. But I can't say Lily having an angle disturbs me. I expect no one to be entirely selfless, and there is something I admire about Lily's constant triangulations and self-marketing—such is the American in me: I can't help but like the man (or woman) forever hustling, and eternally eager to *sell me this pen*.

"Teacher Goble! About my idea?"

My jaw's a little better—likely wide enough to admit two of the locally beloved, thick, chewy, oil-slicked potato noodles at once, rather than the solitary strand I managed a few days before. I'm feeling generous.

"Yes, Lily? What can I do for you?"

"I would like to host a program—a radio show, but in person—at the end of the semester."

"Sounds great, Lily! You'll do a fantastic job."

"You will be the first guest, Teacher Goble."

"Sure...what? Why?" I shudder, not so much from the weather as from the thought of trying to engage a room of listeners for an hour. "I don't have anything to say. You know that!"

"And yet you are a teacher!"

"That's true."

"I do not think you understand your appeal, Teacher Goble."

"That's also true," I await the rest of Lily's elaboration. *Nothing comes.* "Lily?"

"Yes, Dear Teacher?"

"Care to explain?"

"Explain what?"

My ego is tempting me to ask about *my* appeal, even more than about what Lily means by *a radio show, but in person*. What, if any, is the draw to me other than my willingness to play along as a pet, defanged foreigner (a *potbellied capitalist pig, perhaps*)? Could it be that my charms are actually…

"Oh! About the show! Yes, I want to have a program for my students. They would like to learn more about America! You will be the guest of honor!"

I can't imagine what this would entail. Still, Lily's determination ropes me in, and I have agreed to *something* before I have time to consider if I am agreeing to an interview, a presentation, or a public vivisection.

***

Returning to the Château, I greet the guards. Trusting they'd arranged their dinner in the barracks (meaning *my cabinets*), I decide to start mine. Off come the greatcoat and the jacket underneath, and I wash my rice as per Ethan's (meticulously followed) instructions before adding sufficient water to the rice cooker's pot, locking the lid, and turning on the cooker with the *snap* of a switch. A tiny neon indicator lamp—old tech—on the cooker glows orange, establishing that the machine is working.

Under the buzz of the Château's fluorescents, I think about stereotypes and the weight of them. To the extent that I had any of the Chinese, they were benign. And aside from the Chinese being good at math, my preconceived notions were based on what I had heard on RTI or seen in movies.

My father and I were never close, which is not to say we didn't get along. Dad spent most of his time at work, away from the stress and struggle of his legal residence—his *house*.

Home is where the heart is—and Dad's heart was at the office. That was where he relaxed and where he would take my brother and me, both preteens, on occasional sunny Sunday afternoons. There, he could spread out stacks of paperwork on a conference table, sorting originals and carbon copies into piles and merrily work away, his handwriting so bad that only one of the secretaries could read it.

Bureaucracy is magic—it takes all the mess and complexity of industry, commerce, and the human experience and makes all clean and orderly. Thus, each condition is reduced to a checkbox and every cause and explanation to a filled-in line or a dense block of third-person text. And the bureaucrat, an occult practitioner. So it was that my father, a social worker by trade, reduced domestic squabbles fueled by decades of hate to incident reports, custody battles to canary forms, and an alcoholic's spiral to a binder of case notes.

Draw down the gods of triplicate, and all makes sense. A line (and a place) for everything, and everything on its line—*bureaucracy-land* is a dominion of its own, with kings, knights, mages, and peasants, ghosts and superstitions, and it's everywhere and nowhere at once. Away from home or not, I know Dad took comfort in that—in the soft incantations of the *Pencil-Pushers' Grimoire* and its spells for squeezing any problem in the world to flat, letter-sized dimensions.

The office, a three-story former residence built not long after the abolition of slavery, had been neglected for years before Dad's employer bought it dirt cheap. Refurbished to the humble standards of a hanging-on-by-a-thread mental health non-profit, the building had not been gutted, its character partially spared. Thus, it was left with an *impersonal personality* that fascinated me and invited me to snoop, poke, and prod. The decades crashed therein, arranging themselves into something doubly, if not quadruply, antiquated to a boy in the 1990s. Wrought-iron fleur-de-lis boot scrapers outside the brick-stepped entrance stood watch, and oversized fireplaces (still functional, converted to gas logs) framed a workplace of intermittently running IBM XPs and Selectrics. Cabinets filled with microfiche, randomly installed dark wood paneling, and puke-green (avocado) rolling chairs added to the clashing ambiance of mixed formality and styles.

Steam rises from my rice cooker, with the gentle hiss of hard grains turning soft. I catch a whiff of jasmine—no cheap stuff from the bulk barrel here, not in the Château—and I think of heat beating back the damp of my walk and the soothingness of simple carbs.

In the tiny kitchenette next to the conference room on the third floor, my father would hunch over a microwaved Cup Noodle—blowing on every bite till it was no more than a degree or two above room temperature. The old man's persnickety, almost Goldilocks sensitivity to food temperature invited ridicule from *the spouse* (and, in truth, his children, though they were less overt). But at the office, he could enjoy the aroma of powdered bouillon and MSG as he pleased. This modest meal he experienced fully, with a presence that was out of character for a man more inclined to stare absently into the distance. One can speculate as to what the ghosts would think—the men in bowlers, the Hoodoo women, and the disco kids in leisure suits, collars open wide—of this timid indulgence, done in the quiet.

But ghosts keep their own counsel, even around magicians, letting us think of them what we will.

My father's other pleasure: martial arts films. *The Big Boss*, *Enter the Dragon*, *Fists of Fury*, and a clutch of *Bruceploitation* films that I am nearly certain he could not distinguish from those made by the real deal—all were a constant presence at home. And the infrequent weekends my father was neither away from the house nor locked in a downstairs office, paying bills, were spent watching Bruce or the many imitators who arose after his sudden demise. Real Bruce or counterfeit, occasional bad dubbing and blaring horn soundtracks aside, the message was the same—*beat the bad guy, save the innocent, respect your teachers, practice your craft relentlessly*. And that message was *heroic*, sterling, and far removed from the mundane of a life behind a desk.

The fact that all my father's passions—paperwork (or *paper*), instant noodles, and kung fu films—were Asian in origin is not lost on me while I sit on a campus with the Wuling Mountains barely out of view. Packaged, sanitized, sterilized, twice-cooked, and both authentic yet suitable for decontextualization—this is how one readies a cultural product for export, reworking it to survive every type of mixing, modulation, amplification, broadcast, *remixing*, re-modulation, re-broadcast, reception, and reincarnation.

We, Americans, do the same, and I'd be interested in knowing what freeze-dried gunslinger stereotypes my students have of me.

Click! A switch pops up, an indicator light goes off, and the rice is done.

What else to cook? There must be something here—tofu and celery, if nothing else. The next time I'm out, I'll buy a few cups of *Master Kong* instant noodles, to which I'll add a generous portion of chili oil—the kind of heat no amount of blowing, puffing, or waiting can lessen.

My father would absolutely hate them. Months earlier, I might have as well.

***

Green clementines appear at the markets as the weather grows brisker. They won't be ripe for months. But the picking starts earlier—it must. There is such an overabundance of said fruit in Hunan that the local canneries—which produce the vaguely metallic mandarin oranges in syrup in many a Midwestern cupboard (right next to long-since expired La Choy stir-fry mix)—would be overwhelmed if they didn't.

Thus, I have a new favorite snack—with the cheerful sour fruit cutting through the oily spiciness of my treasured hot peanuts, which are seasoned with Sichuan peppercorns that make every bite tingle. And this is the breakfast I have, immediately before my first class. I wash everything down with half a bottle of Wahaha sweet tea—literally *iced red tea* according to the label, but I digress—and finish with a little sliver of betel nut husk.

My stomach, if not fully adapted to local conditions, has been tortured into respectful submission, complaining but rarely.

I am sufficiently wired today to be undisturbed by the gray skies and unseasonal cold as I enter the classroom, just the least bit miffed to discover that the English building is without power. Never one for underdressing, I have layered for warmth—socks, underwear, long underwear, pants, an undershirt, a dress shirt, a jacket, an overcoat, and heavy boots. On some days, I wear a vest and tie as well when I feel especially formal. I am about five kilograms heavier than I would be in a state of nature—a sight sufficiently horrifying for me to scrupulously avoid looking in the bathroom mirror when getting into or out of the shower. I layer thusly to keep the cold at bay—such is the truth, but not the whole truth.

Hulking in an accretion of cloth, I look, if not substantial, at least not frail—not brittle or misproportioned. This is good. And I am a modest person (*in person*, if not in print), puritanically uncomfortable displaying too much of myself. I am not much more eager to reveal my personality, making known my predispositions and opinions to a select few, and slowly.

For all my love of travel, I would rather not show myself at all on as many days as not, communicating from a distance—as a disembodied voice or precisely worded messages. Layers of space and distance salve and soothe my timidity. Nevertheless, I am here and seasonally attired.

Thus weighed down, my arms restricted, I scratch out *problem(s)* and *solution(s)* on the board, picking up where a previous lesson left off. Rain starts to fall outside, first gently, then intensifying to a downpour, as is typical in semi-monsoon climates.

And the room is too dark for instruction. I pat myself down, search through my messenger bag—*nothing*—before turning to my students, hoping someone can help.

One of them dashes away wordlessly and, within a few minutes, returns, emergency candle and matches at the ready. *This could be... painful.* But chin up and back to work! I light the candle and hold the flame close to the chalkboard, gently, trying to avoid dripping wax on my person or coat, and class proceeds—problem and solution alike identified. (The *new problem*—that of my hand being a candlestick with nerve endings—has yet to be addressed.)

The class's momentum slows, likely a product of the chill and darkness, as the students retreat into themselves and droop in their chairs like slowly dying flowers. So I decide to change the topic for a moment (and do some learning of my own).

"Just to check, everyone, raise your hand if I am not the first American you have met."

Crickets and blank stares. I shouldn't have phrased that as a negative, I suppose.

"Let's try again: Raise your hand if you met an American prior to meeting me."

Two hands.

"Okay, you can put those down," I falter for a second, realizing I might well be opening myself up for some unusual feedback, "When you think of an American, what or who comes to mind?"

Ten hands.

"Yes," I point to a woman in back, bundled in a puffy coat, "what do you associate with Americans?"

"Friends!"

"Uh, what kind of friends?"

"On TV, Teacher Goble. Have you seen it? It is very funny!" she lets out a quick giggle.

"Oh! The show!" I was half-expecting this answer—as of 2009, the show is at peak popularity in China. In Beijing, there is a *Friends-themed* café, and there might be others in different cities. The appeal of the program is lost on me; I know *what* is popular, but not *why*.

To me, *Friends* feels oddly archaic—something from a different, more optimistic era—pre-global war on terror, pre-housing crash, pre-social media and endless texting—and a land of coffee dates and answering machines.

My America is one of *I've abandoned my boy!* and *Drainage!* and charlatan-pastors bludgeoned with bowling pins.

My America is a place of high school chemistry teachers learning that the game is rigged and that crime, if done with panache and technical prowess, pays very well.

My America is fathers and sons outrunning cannibal hordes.

My America is paranoid, hallucinating terrorists under every bush and blanket—a nation besieged, born four months after I turned 18, when the September sky above the farm was clear, blue, and pleasingly, if unnervingly, silent, and my father called me and asked if I had seen the news.

My students' America is one of marginally employed waitresses surviving on a single income in New York City.

But stars supernova a million years prior to us seeing their last light, and even the *livest* of live broadcasts ends milliseconds before the final syllable dies in the crackle and hiss.

All that said, the class perks up at the mention of the program, so we'll work with what we have.

"It is great!" another voice chimes in.

"Okay, so raise your hand if you have seen *Friends*."

All hands!

"Okay, raise your hand if you *like Friends*."

One hand—possessed by the only woman to quote Marx in class—lowers. *That figures.*

"Interesting! And what does *Friends* make you think about Americans?"

"They are very humorous!" pipes in one.

"They are active!" goes another.

"They are loud!" announces a third (quite appropriately) as loudly as she can.

"They," *snicker*, "keep finding new boyfriends and girlfriends."

"Great!" I gather my words, looking at the class—the flowers were not dying, but wilting, easily perked up with a ray of sunshine. "What about negative stereotypes? Most of what you have said is positive or neutral. Does *Friends* suggest any problems with America or Americans?"

I could hear a hayseed hit the dirt. No one knows what they can say without offending *Old Teacher Goble.*

"Please, let me know. This is a class discussion." I offer a smile of Mr. Rogers' sincerity. "I assure you that I will not be offended."

A hand in the back is raised with much hesitation.

"Yes!"

"They... they are too energetic," she waits. I smile more broadly than before—*And?* "They are like children!"

"An interesting observation! And I can see how you could come to that conclusion. Anything else?"

"They are not loyal!" *Aw! The Marxist is speaking.*

"And what do you mean by that?"

"They are self-indulgent capitalists who are unsuitable for marriage!"

I am tempted to point out how radically the early Soviets redefined marriage—with everything from *free unions* to nearly instant divorce—but I hold my tongue.

"That's certainly one way of thinking about it!"

My curiosity is getting the best of me, and my next question might well set my firmly planted (and recently revivified) students and *their 100 thoughts to blooming*. I steel myself, determined to take criticism with more grace than did the Great Helmsman.

"Am I what you expect when you think of an American?"

Total. Perfect. Silence.

I stick the base of my candle in the mouth of my now-empty tea bottle—it makes a decent holder and will hold until the candle burns down and melts the plastic.

"I would like your perspective! No pressure! I would like to know for my own sake. That's all."

One brave hand is raised, tentatively—I'll try to remember it. *This kind of heroism deserves some White Rabbit.* I nod in anticipation.

"Not... not really."

"That's okay! How so?"

"You are too serious!"

"I thought I was the paragon of funny!" *haha*, "but understood! Anyone else?"

"You are not tall enough," says a woman who is 1.5 meters tall on a good day.

"Well," I lift myself on tiptoes behind my desk, "I can see your point. Anyone else?"

"You are too thin!"

"I prefer the term *fashionable*, but *thin* works." I keep smiling.

"You are not athletic!"

"I know!" I pretend a sniffle.

"And you are too old!"

"Really? How old do you think I am?"

"Forty!"

"Forty-five at least!"

I am about to wince before I catch myself. *As of today, I am 26, but close enough in the geological scheme of things, I suppose.*

Not so much defeated as surprised, I am learning a lesson in Chinese culture—Chinese honesty is exactly that: no compliment sandwich, no euphemistic phrasing, no honeyed words. And the speed at which a conversation can go from formal circumlocution to absolute directness can be neck-snapping fast. Become truly close friends with a Chinese person, and you may be greeted with a "Oh! You've gained so much weight!" after a perfunctory *nǐ hǎo*.

"So," the candle is burning down, and I remember I am paid for more than sating my idle curiosity, "are you disappointed, pleased, or purely confused at finally meeting an American?"

I wait.

"Anyone?"

I wait. Finally...

"You bring candy," the student says with a smile. I see her classmates nod, and several laugh.

And I suppose that's the important thing.

***

"Brant, hello, what are you doing?" I look up from my phone. *Ethan.* It's been a few weeks since I last saw him, and I was beginning to think he had disappeared.

"Food," I point to a row of sweet potatoes lining the top of a makeshift portable oven. "Thinking about buying a snack."

"I see."

We're standing in front of the gate of the East Campus, where a half platoon of snack sellers has assembled, as they do when the weather permits, around lunchtime. I'm partly bundled up today, with my jacket keeping me warm enough to brave the outdoors. For the sellers, this is the prime business season.

After a brutally negative, gut-clutching experience at a restaurant on the edge of Celestial Lake not long before, I had nearly stopped dining out. This, one might think, would make me doubly unwilling to purchase anything edible from the side of the road. But I've learned caution, not complete avoidance.

From the vendors, nuts, dried fruit, corn puffs extruded from a rattling machine, and fried dough twists were an option, as were *gān wāndòu*—dried hard peas, lightly salted—when my jaw was in working order. I've come to look forward to these treats—rewards to myself for a day spent disabusing my students of any delusions they have of American charm or good looks.

Sweet potatoes, roasted in a converted 55-gallon drum with a welded-in wire grate and a door cut in its side, are a particularly palatable treat. Soft, caramelized through the outer third, and hot enough for steam to rise from one into the bracing air—this is a comfort food of the simplest sort. And cheap!

"Care for a snack, Ethan?" I point to the yam, "My treat."

"No, thanks. I have had my fill of those." Ethan squints at them, ever so faintly disgusted. *Hmm. Who hates sweet potatoes?* And I'm puzzled.

"Oh! So you already had lunch today?"

"No," Ethan shrugs. "I ate them every day growing up, with rice."

"I have that sometimes. It's okay."

"Yes, but, uh...a meal dictated by economics tastes different from one freely chosen."

"I see." *But I don't.* Hunan is hardly as wealthy as the more prosperous parts of the United States, but food prices here are low, low enough that I'm uncertain how the fruit and vegetable sellers stay in business. Still, Huaihua is rough around the edges, so much so that I've seen water buffalo being led down the sidewalk as I sat in a diner eating seaweed soup. A decade ago, all must have been different, and rougher still.

"Where were you raised, Ethan? Huaihua?" An inexcusable oversight on my part—I've never actually asked before.

"No, somewhere much smaller. You should visit," he pauses for a beat, looks at his watch, "Oh! I really need to get going."

"Thanks, Ethan. Maybe I will."

And Ethan's off to the canteen. I'm left gnawing on my potato, wondering if Ethan's journey to Huaihua and the city's, to modernity, for all their differences, were any less circuitous than mine.

***

"Teacher Goble," *Knock! Knock! Knock!* "Teacher Goble!"

I rub my eyes and glance down at my Casio. *08:15, Sunday—Is that who I think...*

"Good morning, Teacher Goble!" *Knock! Knock! Knock!* "Hello!"

Yep!

I cast aside my blanket, roll off my particleboard-hard box spring, and pull on my clothes. I would brush my teeth and comb my hair before receiving a visitor, but...

Knock! Knock! Knock!

"Teacher Goble!"

So I wander to the gate and open it to a sunniness that borders on irritating—some from the heavens and the rest radiating from my perennial guest.

"Hello! You were asleep, Dear Teacher?"

I can hear the lightest touch of reproach in the question, as though everyone should bounce out of bed at the earliest hour and forthwith commence their long march to the canteen. I don't take the bait.

"Astute, as always, Lily, care to come in?" I say the last words to her back. She is now well inside the Château. I close the gate/medium-density fiberboard door. "Can I help you with something?"

"We need to practice for the show!"

"What show?" I call out, befuddled, as I stumble back through my bedroom and into the bathroom. I close the door before brushing my teeth, scouring my face, and combing my hair with as much vigor and velocity as I can manage.

"The ENGLISH SHOW, DEAR TEACHER!"

"Huh?" I glance at my safety razor and rub my poor excuse for a five o'clock shadow—*Maybe later.*

I'm back in the Château's salon in a minute and ready to receive my guest, who is seated and evidently made herself comfortable enough.

"Coffee, Lily?" I flip a red switch on the back of my water dispenser before retrieving a mug from the kitchen, into which I dump a generous portion of Nescafé.

"No! I am young and energetic, Dear Teacher!"

"You don't say?"

"But I do say, Dear Teacher!" *I've thrown her off kilter a bit.*

"Never mind. So what are we doing?" *Sip! And I'm feeling less ghostly.* "And when is the show, uh, program, uh, event?"

"In three weeks!"

"That soon! And what are we doing at this show?"

"Talking!"

"As sometimes happens on talk shows," I take another sip of coffee and pop in a betel nut, "but," *chew, chew, gnaw,* "about *what*?"

"You can talk about your time in China and about life in America." *Okay, this song and dance again?*

"That's it? Do you think people want me to hear me rabbit on about this another time? Won't your audience find it boring?" Lily's face clouds with consternation. She might be ready to admit *Dear Teacher* has a point.

"Maybe you can give me students who want to go to America some advice!" *And just like that, I am every bit as much at a loss as Lily was.*

***

After another hour or so, Lily and I have developed a working plan for the big event. I remain skeptical of Lily's audience projections, even as I am impressed by her ability to persuade/coerce/flatter me into agreeing to participate. And I have been given homework—tasked with finding photos of my home, my family, and anything else to add light and color to our (presumably) pleasant, pre-planned patter. This is *not* an easy assignment, and it causes me to consider the possibility that Lily may be stricter with her charges (or fan club members) than I am with mine. Having no such photos on hand, I must email my family and ask for evidence of a life I rarely thought fit to document.

And then Lily departs, with a *Thank you, Dear Teacher* and *I hope your jaw is better*. I am left alone, uncertain of how to spend the rest of a Sunday that started earlier than I would have liked.

***

My language skills, while still abysmal, have improved to the point that I can buy food, although my pronunciation turns even the simplest request for a price—*Nǐ hǎo, lǎobǎn, duōshǎo qián?* into *Knee-how, lao ban, dough-shao chee-ann?* And my voice—never much to my liking—is somehow *twangier* and more grating in my second tongue than my first.

The proprietress of the West Campus's commissary finds my efforts amusing. She, like many Chinese, is remarkably generous in her assessments of a foreigner's language skills, with even the most mangled pronunciation of basic phrases earning a *Nǐ de hànyǔ hěn hǎo!* (*Your Chinese is excellent!*) and an undeserved thumbs up. This *could* be because the Chinese appreciate pale-faced barbarians learning (however poorly) their language and culture. It *might* be because they fancy their language to be uniquely rich and challenging. Or they *may be* amused by the effort, impressed not by my competence, but that I, like a dog walking on its hind legs, can manage the task at all. I *suspect* the latter but *hope* for one of the former.

Either way, said proprietress gives me tiny discounts—rounded-down totals—as often as not. And it is to her establishment I go not long after Lily's exit, not so much because I have money to spend or need anything, but because I am inclined to browse.

The commissary is in the Fine Arts Building, which gives me an excuse to see the handiwork of the school's wealthiest students. (*Art*, deemed a luxury subject, demands a higher tuition rate than the more strategically important English, science, and engineering.) The building has a correspondingly unhurried air to it, with halls lined with elaborate red paper cutouts, many bogglingly impressive, and students playing friendly games of badminton in the airy courtyard. There are limits to the comfort—no heat and a fine layer of grime on the blue-and-white subway-tile walls—but *luxury* is a relative concept, so the building is *luxurious enough*.

The commissary's stock changes according to the whims of the proprietress and the vagaries of informal supply chains. Aside from the perennial paper, ink stick and grinding stones (*mò tiáo* and *yàn tái*), brushes, pens, and the like, the store, much like a box of chocolates, offers a plethora of curious finds. Lined up on the shelves today are bottled tea, Master Kong noodles, preserved chicken feet wrapped in plastic (probably the most impractical snack I have ever seen), and toilet paper. Atop the display case holding Jinhao fountain pens is a cardboard box of pouches of cherry-flavored *bīng kē*. And behind the case is the proprietress herself—gray-haired and matronly. She smiles.

"*Nǐ hǎo, lǎoshī!*" (*Hello, Teacher!*)

"*Lǎobǎn, nǐ hǎo! Nǐ yǒu bù yǒu wánglǎojí?*" I ask. And *blah, blah, blah.*

So it seems there is no *Wanglaoji*—a soft drink/traditional herbal digestive sold in green Tetra Pak cartons. I *need* nothing, but stomach remedies are good to have on hand. *Hmm, if not that, what should I...*

"Hello, Brant." *Who?*

I turn around, and there stands Ethan, a clutch of other young men accompanying him, all dressed for the outdoors in puffy vests and blue jeans.

"Hello, Ethan!" I look everyone up and down, noting the vests and autumn wear, "How's your weekend going?"

"Fine, my friends and I are going hiking."

"Good for you. I hope you enjoy it." *Wait. Hiking? In the city?* "Uh, where?"

"Zhongpo Mountain."

"I have never heard of it."

"It is close. Would you care to come?"

I think about my day and realize I have nothing planned but sitting in front of a computer in the concrete drabness of the Château, looking for English-language shows on *Tudou*— literally, *potato*, but also one of China's largest video sharing sites.

"Well, I might."

"And there is a temple there, and since you are a Buddhist..."

"Uh, sure, yeah." The truth is that I am *not* a Buddhist, *at least not yet*, but my non-drinking, non-lecherous, vegetarian lifestyle has led many to *believe* I am a Buddhist. The first person to ask me about my religion—Lawrence—did so immediately after I mentioned that I didn't eat meat. Others followed. I corrected them the first ten or twenty times, but that led to a great many questions and perplexed looks, so I became a Buddhist *of sorts* by popular vote—*if he looks like an enlightened duck, and oms like...* "Actually, that sounds interesting. Do you have a minute? I need to go get my coat."

"Take all the time you need." Ethan turns and speaks briefly to his friends in a dialect I can't catch. They all nod in assent. "We'll be at the front gate."

***

Coat on, gloves at the ready, sufficiently bundled, I clodhop my way to the gate with as much grace as my work boots allow to find Ethan and his companions.

"So, how do we get there?"

"We will take the bus." I have quick flashbacks to my first sojourn with Ethan and my later excursion to the train station with my students. I flinch for a second at the thought of another ride subject to *the Mister Gear Destroyer's* grinding whims and mercies or, worse yet, *Lady Death Proof's* rolling stops. I hope no one catches the terror washing over my face.

"Sounds great!"

And so on the bus we go, crammed in, but less than on my previous trips, and one of Ethan's friends offers me a seat.

Three bus transfers—none of them fatal—later, and we are deposited at an inauspicious stop on the dustiest outskirts of our dusty city.

"We're here, Brant."

"Well, *here* is where I usually am." Ethan half-smiles at my statement. "But other than not being *there*, where is *here*? I don't see a park." Ethan points to a walking trail across the road that leads into a stand of trees.

"There is the entrance. So, maybe our *here* is *almost there*."

"I see!"

"Gentlemen, let's go." Ethan addresses us all in English.

***

Almost there proves a term subject to varied interpretation—much like being *a little bit pregnant* or *mostly dead*—and we spend ten minutes walking up an incline that makes my boots bend and creak. I suppose visitors to the United States experience a similar sense of *distance disappointment* when they realize the advertised *short drive* is actually 90 minutes at 200 kilometers an hour. (It's more if one slows down to discharge his pistol into a pedestrian—a customary salutation in the United States—or so the Frenchman is assured.) Yet we prevail, and after what feels like a prolonged retreat from the KMT, we arrive at the entrance of *Zhongpo National Forest Park* (*Zhongpo Mountain*, for short), from whence the *actual* hike can begin.

Walking through an unlocked gate with a guardhouse attached, we are given a once-over by the occupant, an unshod middle-aged man dressed in a forest-pattern camouflage uniform stripped of all insignia. He shortly thereafter returns to tending a wok of noodles boiling over a charcoal flame. *They really do like their gates, don't they?*

Under a chaos of jade and evergreen, the air is sword-sharp and foliage-scented—far removed from the city's island of heat and diesel exhaust. Twisted branches overhead, we start up the path, passing over a rocky stream as the paved trail switchbacks upwards. I am following the pavement, huffing along, until Ethan stops me.

"We are not going that way."

"But there's the road." I nod at the smooth blacktop.

"It is *one* of them. We are taking that way." Ethan points to a dirt path diverging from the main line. "You wanted to see the temple, right?"

I look down at my boots, clean, untouched by muck and grime, and look up to the steepness of the narrow, winding path. *You're committed at this point, buddy.*

"Sure, that sounds interesting."

So we weave up the mountain, splitting from the large dirt trail to a smaller, steeper one. I stop, winded, at a little plateau. Ethan and his friends appear unfatigued, while I resist the urge to clutch my chest and expire.

"What's that, Ethan?" I point to an upright stone mere steps away, pressed into a recessed shelf of earth.

"People used to live here. That's a tomb."

"How fitting." I press a finger against my wrist to check my pulse. *Yep, still got one.*

"What?"

"Never mind," *gasp*, "Anyway, how far is the temple?"

"Very close! We are minutes away." I could point out that the time from the beginning of the universe to the present could be measured in minutes as well (something like 7.26×10^{15} of them, but still...). Nevertheless, I hold my tongue, fearing exhaustion might cause it to wither away and die.

For someone raised on a farm, I am in disastrous shape. This is not by accident. I am *from* the countryside, but was never much (willfully) *of* it. And as tempting as it is to lie and claim my studiousness is the product of a pure, platonic passion for learning, it is not. Rather, it is at least as much a means of escape, not solely to ride the waves and currents of the sky *elsewhere*, but to get away from *hard physical work*. I would rather push a pencil for a month than a plow for a second, and I aspire to avoid having so much as a shrub to trim. No ranch house or white picket fence for me—between my father's time away from the farm and me being the eldest son, I had more than my fill of playing groundskeeper. Years later, I will notice most of my more rustic former students are of the same bent. Virtually to the last woman (and occasional man), they had moved into high-rises and megalopolises, with not so much as a potted plant for company. Hence:

"I'll," *wheeze,* "trust you," *huff,* "on that." *Hack! Cough! Cough!*

The tomb looks more appealing by the moment—too appealing—so we carry on.

As it turns out, Ethan's final assessment was reasonable—another five minutes up a hill, and a clearing with concrete stairs set into the side of a cliff appears. Up those (with a plodding cautiousness), a turn left and onto the plateau, and finally:

The temple!

***

And I stop to breathe, far enough from the stairs to avoid a thirty-foot faceplant if I slip. The group has all assembled.

I look up, seeing Huaihua in the distance, gray high-rises and bright yellow construction cranes lost in the smog. Horns honk faintly—at the lowest levels of human perception—in the distance. I can hear my pulse in my ear, slowing to a leisurely adagio.

I turn around and see a traditional Chinese cauldron with legs (*dǐng*) filled with sand, into which incense sticks had been stuck, long since burned down and cold. Bright prayer flags run along a fine rope from one tree to the next, adding color to the scene. Twenty steps behind the cauldron: a building in red ochre with dragon-carved pillars, a stone porch, open double doors, and the inevitable upturned eaves.

"This is a good temple," offers one of the friends—a tall man in a Columbia Sportswear jacket and Li-Ning sneakers—with studied solemnity.

And I am inclined to agree, if for no other reason than the place's aura. Up here—halfway to the mountain's peak—there's a gentle breeze, and I catch the slightest odor of sandalwood.

"Can we go inside? Is it allowed?" I look to Ethan, well aware of my ignorance of protocol.

"Of course," Ethan stops, speaks to his friends, and I turn back to look at them, my nose pricked with the sharp scent of tobacco. About a third of the crowd have cigarettes dangling from their mouths. *Dear God, I was outpaced by a pack of smokers.* But maybe cigarettes are different in the Eastern Hemisphere—lung fortifying, rather than damaging—something akin to the north-south reversal in the spin of water down the drain. *At this rate, perhaps I should start.*

"After you," Columbia points to the door, and into the temple we go, cigarettes politely dropped and stomped out before anyone enters.

The temple is smaller than I expected—a wide hall, surprisingly shallow, with three large Buddhas, no less than three meters tall, bright with gold foil, each making a different hand gesture (*mudrā*) that I am inclined to believe holds meaning. (As a non-Buddhist/Buddhist, however, I know not what.) There are no monks here, just a geriatric woman, wrinkled and unmoving, sitting to the side of the entrance, wrapped in a blanket. She smiles beatifically, saying nothing. Every step, every whisper, echoes off the walls, which has the paradoxical effect of drawing my attention to how nearly silent the place is. I look up at the elaborate painting of the Buddha on the ceiling, with what appears to my untrained eye to be heaven and hell surrounding him, and I am reminded of the pavilion at the school.

There is a weighty chill to this place—not of physical temperature alone, but of mood, as though the Buddhas are at rest, settled in and content with what has been and what may come. As the calm washes over me, I feel something of the pull of retiring to a temple. The small windows and permanent semi-darkness, the tending of statues and gazing down on the city without hurry—all this appeals to me. And a life without the coarse rush of blood and frustration, one spent waiting for unannounced travelers to come, pay their respects, and move on—this could be reason enough to stay.

We shuffle around for minutes, respectfully doing nothing in particular. I imagine the group—younger, fitter, and more energetic than I am—must be getting bored. I look around, trying not to appear more obviously out of place than is dictated by my awkward, round-eye presence. *Is there a protocol for leaving the temple? Should I do something before I go?*

I consider the totality of my circumstances—from the faintly whistling wind to the eternal stillness of the Buddhas to the increasingly restless presence of Ethan and Co. behind me.

Back on the farm, I had a set of long-tube windchimes, expensive and hand-tuned—purchased with odd-job money when I was a pre-teen—that I hung on the balcony outside my bedroom, next to a lantern. On windy autumn nights when storms rolled through the valley below, I'd hear them ring, their clang and clammer punctuating every gust, catching air on its unhurried way to somewhere better, and watch the kerosene flicker. And *there and then* is somehow *here and now*, at least in the mood of the place. There's continuity in the flow.

This is cinematic, I think—a towering compliment from an American, for whom film is the national literature. I take a clear breath, and the solution presents itself:

I nod my head towards the Buddhas and tip an invisible hat as though I were one cowboy acknowledging another; two men, each going their separate ways. There's something vaguely Kurosawa about this (at least that's the intent).

"Brant, do you want to pay respect to the Buddha?" Ethan asks, his voice barely audible. I glance at the statues again, suspecting the Buddha would appreciate my meaning, if not my delivery.

"I already did."

***

Ethan and the Chainsmokers lead the way up the hill, as we pass by trees that aren't trees—I know I've seen these before, and the joints along the trunks and regular intervals remind me of *something*.

"What are these?" I ask no one and everyone, pointing to the grove, its canopy of thin, sharp leaves towering above us.

"Bamboo," Ethan looks at me askance, "I believe bamboo can be produced domestically in the United States, can it not?"

And Ethan's right: we *do have bamboo*, but the bamboo on the farm (a scaled-down version of the behemoths looming over me) grows less than knee-high. It's one grass amongst many, and not an impressive one.

"It's amazing!" I, slack-jawed (and likely sounding half-witted), point to the tallest one. "I didn't think bamboo could get this massive!"

I hear a good-natured chuckle from the gang.

"We are glad you like it! It is very Chinese!"

As the altitude increases, my fatigue diminishes. Dumbfounded by the bamboo forest and the picturesque spring that weeps water from the mountainside, I am energized. ("Have a try," one of the friends points to water spilling from a pipe bored into limestone—and I do. It's sweet, with a gentle roundness.) Another hour, and we have passed abandoned houses, barbecue pits, and women with carts hawking bottled juice and grilled spiced tofu on skewers. We are nearly at the top.

On the main trail, the crowd is considerable, and the vibe changes from that of *Journey to see the Kung Fu Master on the Mountain* to *Sunday afternoon at the park*. Bicyclists zip by, and the path levels off. The stands of bamboo are behind us, and we pass by well-tended groves of shrubs with thick, shiny leaves and delicate white blooms that perplex me. *Flowers? This time of year?*

"Those are pretty." I point to ones on the hill above us.

"Those are tea plants," Ethan nods, "the cooking oil from them is rare compared to commodity oils."

"You cook with oil from tea?" *Ugh!* "That sounds terrible."

And herein is an issue of vocabulary—*tea oil* is a literally accurate translation of the Chinese (*chá yóu*). Yet the plant in question is different from (but related to) that used to make the scalding torture tea that has burned away half the nerves on my tongue.

Similar but different.

Language is a temperamental beast, each tongue neurotic in its own way. The English speaker must forever track gender and subject/object—*he, she, him, her*—and irregular verbs. Spoken Chinese ignores both, with the endearingly simple *tā* covering all personal pronouns (and *it* to boot!). Yet Chinese inflicts a cruelty of its own, demanding distinction between younger/older siblings and paternal/maternal lines—granularity an English speaker would likely find irrelevant. Thus, we're taught which details matter.

We come to believe we think with precision *where it counts*, the unarticulated extraneous, and marvel at others' inability to see what we *mean* through the miasma of ill-formed thoughts and unexamined intent. Consider *friend*—with a meaning stretched thin from acquaintance to blood brother. I think of *Friends* and wonder how seriously my students take it. *Do they imagine I have friends like that in America? Do they think I should?* In truth, here in Hunan, I have more friends (or at least friendly associates) than ever before.

"Oh, it's not that kind of tea," Ethan answers. "It's quite mild."

And it is—light gold, with a delicate nutty flavor, but too expensive by far for me, so I'll taste it infrequently. *Wealthy American* or not, I'm too poor for fine dining.

Pale amber and azure—that's the sky overhead, with the afternoon sun streaming down. We reach the mountain's plateau and discover a proper park, with picnicking families scattered across the field. Next to it, there's a fenced-off area with a parabolic antenna several meters across and masts bristling with cellular antennas and microwave repeater horns.

Huh, what a thing to find up here!

But I shouldn't be surprised. This vantage affords a long view of the horizon. I wonder if the repeater signals are unencrypted, remembering nights spent on the farm and the spiring tower behind it, a lone red light atop it pulsing with a slow incandescent rhythm. Tune one receiver to 800-and-something megahertz (narrow FM), and the other to the correct shortwave channel, and hear versions of the same drawling, preaching voice—one from the nearby repeater, the other milliseconds behind—the time to boomerang from Kentucky to the shortwave transmitter in Florida and back again at the speed of light. This was the feed to WYFR—the same WYFR on which I had listened to Radio Taiwan for hours every night.

Back and forth and back again.

***

An hour on the mountaintop, and we've seen all there is to see. Blue skies and big antennas have their appeal, but I'd rather be on the move, and Ethan and the Chainsmokers seem to think the same. The trip down is comparatively easy. Gravity works that way, regardless of country. Although if I am careless, I might end up tripping and rolling down the road—a fast descent, but likely not the most pleasant one.

We pass by the temple again, and I get a better look at it. Construction material is scattered around, and I take more details of the place—still calm, still removed, but messy, less ideal than I would remember.

"Why is all this here?" I point to the debris. Ethan stops.

"The temple is new. It's not finished yet."

"I guess I assumed this was ancient."

I'm not entirely wrong—*a temple* has been since time immemorial, but not *this one*. Build, destroy, rebuild. The temple is persistent, a phoenix of the Western sort, but different with each rising from the ashes, grander than it was before. Weather, fire, Communists, thieves—they win in the moment of destruction, but lose the war against the persistence of a thing living in memory and then wood and then memory again.

So it is with the Buddhas, too, embodying *upekkhā*—calmness in the face of gain and loss—knowing they'll return—

be here in some form or another—no matter how many times the temple burns to the ground.

And I'll be here again as well, I have little doubt, assuming I don't get lost along the way.

***

With about as much wisdom as giving a toddler an M60 loaded with a belt of ammo and bolting out of the room, the university administration has left me unsupervised. Aside from when I was handed a schedule (and a later meeting in which my passport, with the residence permit sticker affixed, was returned to me), we have had no communication regarding my status or professional duties.

I still lack an official class roster, a policy handbook, or any details about the subject I'm assigned to teach. Said directly, I am not much less ignorant of my role in the school than I was on the day I arrived.

Public Speaking is the course *in practice*, but I could be formally listed as instructing *Western Culture, American Geography,* or *Potato Farming for Fun and Profit*.

In theory, there's no difference between theory and practice. In practice...

Never one to enforce rules no one bothered to tell me, I have become accustomed to students popping in at random, some for a single session, some for a week, and some for a month. Some offer no explanation for their presence. Others tell me they are from a different department and are looking for an opportunity to improve their English. Others still assert that they could hear my twangy bellow from across the hall and were curious whether I deserved my reputation. (*What this reputation is has yet to be explained to me.*)

Being game, I treat these wanderers as informal auditors and invite them to join in with the group activities, give extemporaneous speeches, and otherwise participate. Thus, it is with little surprise that I catch sight of a woman with a sour face and drab apparel in the back of the classroom on a crisp Monday morning.

"Morning, everyone!" I take a sip of black rice congee through a straw. It's a surprisingly pleasant breakfast, recommended to me by a student not long ago—and gentler than black coffee and betel nut.

"Good morning, Teacher Goble."

"Did we survive our weekend?" I smile.

Yes! I suppose, and *more or less* ring out, with one brave smart aleck calling out *No, I'm a ghost, Teacher Goble.*

Such dedication!

"Are we happy to be back in class?"

I can hear the audible equivalent of a shrug.

I catch a half-smirk flashing across the aforementioned sour face. *She seems rather old to be a student. Who? ... Is that Dour Dean?*

I would ask if the Dean needs anything, but then... *If she wants to audit the lecture, why not?*

"Okay, today we are going to discuss our upcoming trial. First, let's talk about crime."

I start by scratching out ideas on the blackboard in my spidery rectilinear script—robbery, murder, arson, and kidnapping—to see what piques the students' interest.

"Which of these crimes sounds most fun to you?"

I hear a murmur in the class and the occasional interjection. There's shape to the comments, but no meaning—*mimoids* and simulacra forming on the surface of Solaris. And at this early hour on the first/worst day of the week, I will consider myself lucky if a half-dozen students volunteer so much as an uncoerced syllable.

"Okay, then, let's all name our favorite crime. We'll start at the back. You there, *new student*," I point to the Dour Dean, and half the class turns around, sees her, and laughs nervously, "Which of these is the best crime for our trial?"

Nothing. Dour Dean hasn't been paying attention.

"Let's phrase it this way: Which of these crimes do you think would be the most interesting?"

"Huh," she sighs, deciding to play along, "Bank robbery, I suppose."

"A pragmatic choice! Next!"

I poll the rest of the class—the Dean's choice was a natural one (or no one dares to disagree).

Bank robbery, it is.

From there, we discuss the mechanics of the crime— *Which bank? How much money? Should the criminal use a weapon?* In all this, the students are engaged: Crime, even in the safest of societies, is an eternal topic. And the extraordinary popularity of *Prison Break* likely adds to the appeal. Of the many unexpected (and occasionally questionable) teaching choices I have made during my first semester as *Teacher Goble*, adding a mock trial as a group activity seems to be proving one of the best.

The class ends. Most hurriedly disperse—off to study Brontë or, curiously, Allan Bloom.

One *student* remains, patiently waiting for the room to empty before approaching my desk.

"Dour...ugh, *Dean*, good to see you. You look well," *I'm lying*. Dour Dean is so ethereally pallid that I fear she may dematerialize if I breathe hard in her direction. *Or maybe she looks great for a corpse.*

A wan smile, and then, "Thank you, Mr. Goble. Your classes seem to be developing."

"As always! As usual!"

"I see," she takes a moment to weigh her thoughts. "Since you are Buddhist," her voice is hushed, without authority, "would you be interested in helping me revise some of my lama's writings?"

"Sure!" I'm eager enough to offer my assistance; making a friend in administration might be advantageous for next semester's research project.

But how am I going to bullshit my way through this one?

"That's great! We can begin tomorrow," and the Dean departs.

What was that?

Was the Dean… *happy*?

***

Days later, Lily catches me after my morning class as I go for lunch at *Allen Coffee*, my regular haunt. With comfortable booths, subdued lighting, decent coffee, affordable vegetarian noodles, and a boss who lets me stay for hours, the café has become my second Château (minus the scurrying guards). My affinity for the place being well known, students appear as they please, seeking midday meetings with me, making my time there very nearly *office hours.*

"Lily! How are you?" I'm in a decent mood, but I'm not going to break stride. Lily walks apace.

"Good morning, Teacher Goble. Are you going for lunch?"

"Yep!" We are at the East Campus's gate. I prepare to dart across the road.

Lily follows me, chatting away as we bolt, then stop, then bolt again across the road—a dance to the halting beat of the *Don't Get Flattened* waltz, recognizable to anyone who's lived where there are no traffic laws, only suggestions. And in a minute, we settle into my well-padded booth. I'd thank *Allen* for keeping it open for me if I knew he was real.

"Care for some lunch, Lily?" I point to the menus tucked into a stand at the table, diner-style.

The boss, a polite woman, soft spoken in the extreme, nicely dressed, comes over. I order from memory. Lily skims the menu and waits a beat before resuming:

"No, Teacher Goble! Your tastes are... too expensive."

A plate of noodles is 12 yuan—about two dollars—and a *Bāxī kāfēi* (Brazilian coffee) is the same. *Am I being scolded?* But I hold my tongue. I could point out that part of what I'm paying for is a reprieve from the cacophony and din of the cheaper restaurants in Hunan, where customers *holler* their orders from across the room and express their occasional dissatisfaction no less directly. But my appreciation for *quiet* might be lost on the present company.

"Dear Teacher!"

"Shhh!" I raise a finger to my lips with studied theatricality, "You'll scare the owner, Lily!"

"Oh!" *stage whisper*, "very sorry, Teacher Goble. Anyway, I have a question for you."

"Ask away."

"What do you think we should name our show?"

"Okey-dokey, let me think." I am flummoxed. *What's in a name? And what am I naming?* Then it occurs to me. "Lily, I have the perfect one in mind!"

***

Thus, the *Okey-Dokey English Show* was born. Selling Lily on the moniker took half my lunch break, but after extolling its virtues, I won. *Okey-Dokey* was gently enthusiastic, none too serious, and promised effort rather than perfection.

I know Lily is preparing for the Show, and I receive updates from her on the event's status every few days. Posters, a red banner, and the occasional flier—I see signs of Lily's handiwork. Not long before the *big event*, I have acquired enough photographs—some from the farm, some personal, some stock—to illustrate a life that Lily seems to consider worthy of inspection (although I have my doubts).

Meetings with Dour Dean go better than planned. The proofreading is light work—not essays, just aphorisms and enigmatic phrases. Pop into Dour Dean's frigid office, skim the provided text, claim comprehension of its implications, tweak it enough to shift a reader's confusion from *befuddlement* to mere *c-fuddlement,* and be on my way. Such becomes a twice-weekly event. And I am learning as I go. *Education by osmosis*, while alien to a man whose youth was spent with his nose buried in books, is haphazard but not ineffective. My hikes to the mountain, where I gaze in awe at the relentless growth of the bamboo groves and enjoy the temple's peacefulness, contribute to my knowledge of the practice, if not the theory, of my assumed beliefs.

Time passes. Finally, Lily's big day (or night) arrives.

***

After nearly a semester on campus, I am still a wandering know-nothing—the hapless haunting spirit of an explorer who fell off the edge of the world—as ignorant of the names and functions of most buildings as when I arrived. Lily—forever anticipating my navigational ineptitude—appears at the gate of the Château on a Thursday evening with an autumn sky that faded from deep purple to black.

"Hello, Dear Teacher! Are you ready for your presentation? I think there will be a considerable crowd!"

"Uh," *and a disappointed one too, if I'm the highlight of the evening*, "Ready enough, Lily." I grab my flash drive, wave to the guards, and we are on our way.

The campus is very nearly noiseless after dark, and *dark* it is. In America, universities, parking lots, and convenience stores are bathed in mercury-vapor light, turning the skin green and sickly and keeping birds chirping at all hours. But here the lights are few and far between, their orange glow and hum dotting the campus at infrequent intervals. It's scarcely enough to allow us to see the way from one lonely island of brightness to the next. A decade from now, whole cities in China will pulse and throb, with light of every color racing up buildings and their millions of LEDs and pouring into the streets. But that's a different kind of lighting—more spectacle, less fear than its stateside counterpart, harsh and joyless, intended to keep thieves and perverts at bay.

But for the present, in Huaihua, *darkness*.

We're at the gate and on a bus, and the night driver seems less hurried—no gear-grinding fury, no *Mad Max* dash from Lord Humungous. Thus, I enter the East Campus with a clear head and clean underwear, Lily chatting up the event as we march towards the Business Building. She has not yet seen the crowd, having left greeting the audience members to one of her assistants while retrieving *Dear Directionless Teacher* from his abode.

We arrive at our destination, which is immediately beside the English building and mirrors its design and layout.

"Oh! This is where we're going! I could have found this on my own."

"Are you sure about that, Dear Teacher?" I can almost hear Lily smiling as she awaits my reply.

"Ugh," *sigh*, "Fair point."

Up the stairs we go, through a building that is lit with little more than starlight; our steps echo, and I hear a murmuring, faint at first, but growing louder as we approach. There's something off. *That... doesn't sound like much of a crowd.* But I could be wrong.

***

And then we're in the room—*I think*, but the fluorescents blind me for a moment, and I could be *anywhere*, in this realm or the next. The lights overhead are a marvel of suboptimal illumination, both plenty bright to dazzle someone coming in from the night and dim enough to strain the eyes of the acclimated, fairly and equitably punishing all and sundry.

Adjusting, I can make out the room, decorated with a banner, but sparsely populated. There can't be more than a dozen people here. I steal a quick look at Lily, quickly, trying to avoid being too obvious. She's still smiling. Lily usually is, but this can't be what she expected.

"Let's wait a minute, Lily."

We sit down in hard folding seats, Lily looking around, me still trying to figure out how much time I need to kill and how thoroughly I need to torture the audience on Lily's behalf with my droning. We chat. I can feel the cold clawing up my legs from the seat, and the audience—what we have of one—is stirring with boredom.

We've waited several minutes, but no one else has arrived.

"Let's get started, Lily."

Lily stands up, pulls down the screen, turns on the projector, and introduces me. *Welcome, everyone! This is Teacher Goble. Blah, blah, blah...*

I shuffle to the front, my hands half-frozen.

There's something forced about trying to describe the mundane, the unremarkable, or even the overly familiar. You grow oblivious to everyday experiences until suddenly you aren't—until something rattles you awake.

The bumpkin's first day in the big city is an adrenaline rush—every jewelry store sparkles, every sports car roars, and every burn barrel and herky-jerky junkie cracks and pops and reeks of something awful. The bumpkin will remember the coarseness of every fiber, every soot-coated hand reaching out to beg, as though they were lasered into the back of his eyelids. And the city slicker nearly jumps out of his skin at the lowing of a cow and hops about like an idiot at the sight of a wheel gun on a good old boy's hip.

Five years in and life's a blur—man can adjust to anything, any joy or terror, and think nothing of it. Then it hits you, as it does from time to time: *My God, I'm here, not there.* And *here* and *there*—wherever *there* was—the from and to—are not the same.

The old country stays gray, ancient—impossible to make interesting.

Nevertheless, I try:

Yammer. Point to the screen. (Audience: *Ooh! Aww!*) Paw at the keyboard with dead hands.

Next slide.

Yammer. Point to the screen. (Audience: *Ooh! Aww!*) Paw at the keyboard.

Next slide.

Yammer. Point to the screen. (Audience: *Ooh! Aww!*) Paw at the keyboard.

Next slide.

And for all my tedium, the audience, what little there is of it, is attentive, politely feigning fascination at photographs of the farm, lakes, trees, and the downtown of a wide spot in the road I can't imagine anyone stopping long enough to notice. I am cheerfully interrupted as often as not to answer questions, ranging from the sensible:

Teacher, what did you grow on your farm?

"Hay and disappointment, mostly."

Huh?

To the off-the-wall:

Did you ever try noodles in Kentucky? Do they have them?

"Yes, and yes. And we eat them with cheese sauce."

Half the room gives me a traumatized look—the Chinese, with a few uniquely worldly exceptions, do not love cheese.

What about rice?

"We have that with butter."

What?! (And from appalled expressions, I realize I may well have insulted a national icon—spit on a statue of Chairman Mao, as it were.)

To the gently simple:

Do American people know what bamboo is?

"Sure, it's something you buy in cans."

To questions about my family:

You have a brother and sister? Is that allowed in America?

"More or less. Children are like cars, you can have as many as you can afford, but if you don't make your payments, they get repossessed."

Really?

"Not exactly, forget that last part."

My answers, while of questionable sincerity, keep the audience from fleeing, and the truthful ones seem to elicit more incredulity than their less plausible peers. *A repossessed child is one thing, but cheese noodles, a different (and more horrifying) matter.* And for all my jocularity, I'm mindful of how absurdly naive my questions about China would be had I not moved here and seen the place firsthand.

I close by thanking the audience for their forbearance and wishing them a life free from rice buttered without the diner's consent.

And then I'm done.

Somehow, I've spent 30 minutes talking about nothing, nowhere, and no one, and I've held my micro crowd's attention to the end.

"Thanks for attending, everyone, and if you have any extra questions for Teacher Goble, he will be here to answer them. Won't you, Teacher Goble?"

"Sure," *Put me on spot, why don't you?* "I'd be happy to stick around."

I pass out my phone number and social media account information to anyone who asks, and after another 20 minutes of good-natured interrogation, the students are gone.

Lily and I are left alone in the room, with the lingering, booming silence of an empty church or a party that has finished, only traces of heat and respiration left behind.

On the way back to the Château, Lily is preternaturally, uncharacteristically untalkative. Crossing the East Campus and its smooth blacktop, I point to the bare brick and concrete skeleton of a hotel rising from a rice paddy across the street.

"That's new! I think it will be impressive!"

"Probably so, Teacher."

"How many stories do you think it will be?"

"I'm not sure."

We're back across another campus, and we finally arrive at the Château. Lily walks me up the stairs. I'm inside and about to close the door when I turn back to her.

"I think that went well, Lily," I hesitate, thinking of what else I could say—something truthful. "The students seemed to have thoroughly enjoyed it."

"Really?" I can see her expression warm a bit.

"Absolutely! You did a good job."

"So did you, Dear Teacher!"

"Well, okey dokey, Lily. We've done enough tonight. I'll see you soon."

Lily smiles at that. We bid each other adieu, and Lily is on her way.

The lightest breeze pushes its way through a kitchen window, and I contemplate the possibility that the weather will turn miserable. I shudder, and the overheads flicker, their subdued rays draining blood from my complexion.

Now it's time for tea.

***

I wake up with a start, cold, my shirt soaked with sweat. It's three in the morning, and the Château's air is mausoleum-still. The guards are on patrol, padding about with admirable stealth.

The semester is drawing to a close, with only review and final presentations remaining (Lily's show was some time ago). I have accumulated what seems to be enough documentation of my work—a syllabus, samples of student work, photographs of student activities and blackboard scrawlings, examination sheets and rubrics, and a report outlining my first semester as a teacher—to submit to my professor. But uncertainty and the looming due date hang over me, the sword's tip scraping my neck. *Better too early than too late.*

I think the sole step left is organization, which should take no more than four hours. I look down at my Casio—03:00. *And I don't need to be on the shuttle until 07:30.*

So I throw off my blanket, salute the quickly dispersing guards, make a cup of Nescafé, and I'm at my desk.

I've never been one to assume good fortune—to accept *it'll all work out*. And I'll never understand how anyone could. I imagine all the little pieces of the modern, electric world and the precarity with which they are held together. And I fear entropy and the chaos-starved goblins of bad wiring and careless installation will conspire against me.

Hard drive, screen, CPU, modem, keyboard, wires, and thousands of kilometers of glass filaments stretching across the mountains and plains, plunging into the sea, and emerging a continent away—I depend on them all. If so much as one link in the chain breaks, I may well be stuck begging for an extension.

The better part of a decade later, I'll be back in the States and wake up on an even colder morning in March, seven hours before my 09:00 dissertation defense, bundle up, pack up two flash drives and a laptop, scooter to the 24-hour study hall, and wait. Hands tingling, mouth full of copper, I'll pace until dawn, considering the many catastrophes that might befall me (or my committee members) on the three-minute walk across campus.

I'll pass, and a friend watching my prattling performance from the back of the conference room will ask me after the fact how I managed to stay as calm as I did. *Practice*, I answer. *Practice faking it* is the truth, but practice nonetheless.

Several hours in, and nothing has caught fire. The computer's fans whir and groan erratically, but work progresses. I sweat even as I shiver. I shouldn't be this nervous, but I am. I stop for coffee, run to the bathroom, and put on an extra layer—these inefficiencies slow me down, and with every peek at my computer's clock, my chest incrementally tightens.

But by 07:15, I have survived the night and compiled a PDF—carefully organized, illustrated, and indexed. There's nothing left to do but log in to my university email account and hope an electromagnetic pulse or a lightning strike doesn't annihilate my work in the next 120 seconds.

Dear Professor, I have attached the complete documentation of my teaching. Let me know if you spot any catastrophic errors or deficiencies. I'd be happy to... blah, blah, blah.

I reread the message, checking it for obvious errors. *Good enough is good enough*, I suppose. I inhale, hold my breath, and wait for my hand, acting too slowly and of its own lurching accord, to move the cursor.

Send!

The email disappears, and I am back to my inbox. My file is on a server on a campus far away, waiting for the sun to rise half a day later than it does here, and for a professor I have never met to read about my struggles to teach a subject I barely know in a place I have not long been. But I don't have the time to think about this.

I'll miss my ride if I don't hurry, so I turn off the computer, fill my thermos with coffee and cane sugar, and scramble out the door, teeth unbrushed, hair half-combed, and coat rumpled.

Settling into my seat on the shuttle, my heart slows as I soak up the cabin's warmth and shake off the wintertime bone-damp. *That's it? That's a semester of work? That's what I achieved?* It's the same hollow feeling I'll have when I hold my diploma in 2010, underwhelmed by the fruit of my efforts.

Still, I should buy some candy for the morning classes. A celebration with the students whose patience allowed me to finish my practicum is called for, and by sharing a little sweetness and good cheer with them, I might get a taste of my own.

***

The last session of the semester—the final Friday—is abuzz with *school's-(almost)-out* energy. I'm in four layers, looking every bit the part of a penguin, waddling and pacing as I explain the final examination protocol.

"Okay, everyone! Here's how this will work: I know your team names. You'll come up to the front of the class, introduce yourselves, state your contribution to the team, and present! This is the rubric I'll be using to assess you!" I point to a one-page form with a percentage breakdown of the grade—the students have seen this, but I might as well jog their memories.

"Remember! Everyone on the team needs to do something to earn a full mark. If you don't speak, fine, but let me know what you *did* do. Who wants to go first?"

And the classroom falls stone silent, as though I were assembling a team to put out fires at Chernobyl.

"Anyone? Anyone? Bueller?"

"Who's Bueller, Teacher Goble?"

"Great question! And thanks for volunteering!"

"Huh?"

It dawns on the student that she (and, by extension, her team) has been *had*—and there's no way to rabbit out of the snare. If she could tuck her ears in closer to her head, she would. She can't, so she narrows her eyes and pulls down her cap.

"Hey, think of it this way: The first to start is also the first to be done!"

"Isn't that what you call *cold comfort*, Teacher Goble?"

So something did stick! Hooray! And I'm practically beaming.

"And such an *apropos* term!" I rub my gloved hands together, dramatically, exaggerating my (very real) shivering. "I'm certain you'll do fantastically!"

The student lets out the faintest *sigh*, stands up, and motions for the rest of the gang to follow.

***

The presentations—for fitness centers, restaurants, at-home jewelry-making ventures, mountain-touring companies, and a smattering of late-aughts e-commerce undertakings selling everything from traditional medicine to snacks—are *surprising*ly good. If a cowboy is waiting to shoot his way out of every American suburbanite to freedom, there's a businessman in every Chinese student, no less eager to bargain his way to generational prosperity. *Stereotypes*, these certainly are, but that doesn't mean they are without a grain of truth.

And before long, we're done. The students depart, on their way to lunch, another final, and then a break from the grind of school.

I'm left alone with a stack of papers, breathing in the chalk dust, and wondering what grade I would give myself.

***

The finals are over when I nearly pass by Dour Dean without noticing her as she walks across the bridge over Celestial Lake. There's a little work left—grading papers and submitting a few reports, but nothing challenging. I've spent most of the last week locked in the Grand Château, typing scores into spreadsheets and cross-checking student names and numbers. I don't mind being inside for a while—I've furnished my apartment enough to be comfortable, adding a few lights—but eventually, the walls start to close in on me. And the guards are likely coming to find my never-ending presence more bane than blessing. With that in mind, I wrap myself in my coat, jam the painfully small matching ushanka onto my head, and step outside under a crystal-blue sky. Thus:

"Dean? How are you?"

"Oh! Teacher Goble?" She's startled, her reverie—her relentless stare into *something*, something far away—is broken.

"How far along are you in your grading?"

"All but done." She half smiles. "And I heard you were doing something related to a graduate degree?"

"That's finished, Dean!" And returned too—I passed. *Apparently, my professor had more confidence in my teaching than I did.*

"So are you returning to America for Spring Festival?"

I've been asked this question before, and I'm tempted to reply with a question of my own—*How could I afford a round trip to the United States on my pittance of a salary?* But I don't. The Chinese, including some of the best educated, assume Americans have considerable family money. (*Ha! Ha! Ha!*) And why ruin an otherwise pleasant chat?

"No, I think I'll stay here."

"In Hunan?" There's a touch of disbelief in the Dean's voice.

"Well, on campus." I shrug.

"But everyone will be gone. There'll be nothing for you to do."

"That sounds fine to me."

Dour Dean's smile fades at my reply, and while we're hardly close, I've grown to like her enough to flinch instinctively, if imperceptibly, at the sight of her disappointment. *But what are foreigners supposed to do, anyway?* "Maybe I'll go to Hong Kong!"

And she brightens again.

"I suppose that would be interesting for you!"

"And what are your plans, Dean?"

"Me?" She wrinkles up her face before catching herself, "I," *pause, pursed lip,* "I suppose I'll visit my husband's family," *sigh,* "I do hope you enjoy your trip."

"Thanks, Dean. I appreciate it." I'm getting cold—winter creeps up on the man who stands still. Dour Dean, rock still in her thin jacket and apparently immune to (or accepting of, as a good Buddhist should be) suffering, nevertheless notices mine.

"Perhaps you should be on your way."

"I'm fine," *chatter-chatter,* "but I suppose," *brrr,* "I should do some shopping."

I stick out my hand, gloved but slightly numb. We shake, and I'm on my way, boots thumping over the bridge, until…

"Teacher Goble?"

I turn around.

"Yes, Dean?"

"There's a closer store that way." She points up a hill.

"Fantastic!" *Nod, nod, brrr.* I'm ready to start jogging.

"And Teacher Goble."

"Yes, Dean?"

"Thank you for your help with the translations."

I nod, smile, my head bobbling and my body shivering as I set off for warmer spaces.

***

Students throng the campuses' gates, crowd onto buses, and disappear.

And everything is quiet for a while, ringing with the same empty-classroom voidness I remember from the end of Okey-Dokey. Most of the teachers are gone as well. Ethan invited me to his hometown again—a place I can't find on a map, but that he assures me is not much more than a stone's throw away from the birthplace of the Chairman. *Maybe later.* Rural Hunan sounds interesting, but my meeting with Dour Dean inspired me. I've budgeted enough to see the Pearl of the Orient, a place about which I know nothing aside from what I learned from Shaw Brothers films. *How does one do a flying side kick? Should I practice before I go?*

The question at hand: *What to do before my trip?* I've scheduled my comprehensive examination for a few weeks from now. I can think of no better time to spend seven days answering essay questions than Spring Festival, and no better place than a campus free of distractions.

As for the Festival itself, I know it entails fireworks, with the culmination—the Chinese New Year—demanding considerable quantities of the most fearsome sort. These can be had by the wheelbarrow-full for shockingly reasonable prices at any number of stores lining the road between campuses.

That said, *demanding fireworks* doesn't narrow things down much in China.

Opening a store? There's nothing like firecrackers to bring good fortune!

Child graduating from college? What better way to show the world the heights to which he'll fly than with a whistling, whining, booming volley?

Grandfather die? Detonate a few hundred barrels of gunpowder to keep the evil spirits at bay!

Have a headache? No? Well, you do now! And what better way to take your mind off it than strapping a fountain to your skull and burning away your pain (and hair)!

There is no event in China that doesn't warrant blowing up something, and no day that couldn't be improved with a healthy dose of gunpowder and tinnitus.

To a boy in the countryside, fireworks were a treat, with the nearby prison farm's July 4th show an exercise in irony. Aerial shells flew over the confines of the barbed wire fence and guard towers, bursting and blossoming midair—celebrations of independence and freedom, launched by men who had neither for an audience that was all too happy to keep them that way. Such were more innocent days and nights.

But a few thousand explosions later, and I've got some ideas as to where that rocket should go.

Fortunately, the real katzenjammer and commotion won't start for weeks, with intermittent *booms* until then. In the meantime, I can relax and admire the *dēnglong*—the round red lanterns with golden tassels hung from the West Campus's gate and the trees along its main boulevard. One thing to remember—I'll need to stock up on food. Students have advised me that all the restaurants will be closed, their rolling shutter doors pulled down. And a single convenience store within walking distance will remain open. My loyal guards and I will be back on the pepper peanut diet if I don't prepare. And none of us—neither highborn nor commoner—should be reduced to that.

So I start making trips from the Château to Jiawei and back.

***

Within a week, the campus is *completely* dead. The other foreigners have departed—some for home, others to visit their Chinese in-laws—and I am left with the guards as my sole company.

The Grand Château is grandly quiet, and I—the *Baron of Befuddlement*—have nothing to do.

I can breathe.

It's not until I've been alone for a few days that I realize how tightly wound I've become—not with unhappiness, not with regret. This is the jittering, pent-up anxiety of someone overwhelmed by novelty, my nerves an induction antenna, electric, a copper coil oscillating and resonating with every frequency and from all directions.

So there's nothing left for me to do but drink.

By *drink*, I mean *drink* torture tea (to stave off the cold), orange juice (to test if the tea burned away my ability to taste sour), over-sweetened coffee (to give me energy—and *indigestion*), *Wanglaoji* (to cure said indigestion), and assorted phosphates, punches, and Fantas of every color of the rainbow.

Walking through the West Campus gate well past nightfall, I see the watchman—green jacket, red armband—his feet in a heated bamboo box. He looks up, points his flashlight at me, and shrugs. *Go ahead.*

I turn off the main route, past the hanging lamps, and their cheerful red and gold light dims with every swallowed step. Soon, I'm in darkness, somewhere near the low-slung international office, with its crumbling pebble facing and—*There's the ATM!* I see the glow of the screen.

Should have bought a candle, Dear Teacher!

And Lily, were she here, would be correct. But she isn't. So I stop and wait in the void, knowing my eyes will adjust well enough for me to pad my way home. Slowly, I begin to make out the trees and see the ramp to the concrete basketball court. If I'm careful, I should be able to avoid dropping the many bottles I'm carrying with me or breaking my leg.

Then I'm meters away from home, having made my way down a *second* ramp with not so much as a stubbed toe, when I look up into a moonless sky and see a faint orange glow above me. *Stars?*

But they're moving.

And there's another. And another. And another. *I know these things—they're Kǒngmíng*—lanterns made of an ivory paper shell and wire, a flame held in place beneath it—hot air balloons in miniature.

They rise, their warm flicker shrinking by the moment, dragged and spun along a gentle zigzag by the layered currents of wind. *What? Where are they coming from?*

I look across the black water of Celestial Lake, and I can barely make out silhouettes on the soccer pitch on the other side. *Who? Students? I thought I was alone here.* But I'm not.

There are fish in the lake, the watchman in his shack, my loyal guards forever at their posts, and the lighters of the lanterns celebrating their break from the humdrum and academic, maybe from the travails of farm and family life as well.

It seems I have as much company as I could want.

The lantern flames won't last for long. Soon, they'll run out of fuel, burn out. They'll crash into a field, cold and useless. But until then, they'll see a little of the world. I smile for them, wishing them a journey worth remembering as they rise into the darkness. I smile for the silhouettes as well, hoping they enjoy their night.

The clamminess of winter has worked its way through my coat, and my feet are getting cold. I'll be back in the Château soon, eating steaming noodles with chopsticks wielded by numb hands as clumsy as seals' flippers.

The mind splits up—attention scatters, attending to every curiosity, wandering through walls, leaving energy and ectoplasm behind—and then returns, bringing mysteries from all parts. So it is with me and my memories—radio waves and hammered jaws, bamboo groves and betel nuts, bright bridges and dark rooms—pulled and pushed by chance, curiosity, and the charm of persistent friends. This is as cohesive as I can be. This is how my stories tell themselves.

I'll be gone from here in a few semesters, off to different cities, different countries. I may never return. But I'll remember this night and this place and my loyal guards and the students who likely couldn't see me in the shadows, and their silent celebration. This is when I took to the sky and floated freely amongst the winds and waves, found company and awesome things and places I never thought I'd see, far away from home—more *at home* than I'd ever been before.

I'll think back and feel this same communion from time to time—a rolling wave of heat, a little zap in my tooth—a ghost of *me*, still standing there, waiting in the cool and dark.

For everything and everyone to come together.

About the Author

Brant von Goble is a writer, editor, publisher, researcher, teacher, musician, juggler, and amateur radio operator. He received a Doctor of Education degree from Western Kentucky University in 2017. During his doctoral studies, he investigated the impact of motivational training on students' social and emotional development.

www.ingramcontent.com/pod-product-compliance
Lightning Source LLC
Chambersburg PA
CBHW050520100526
44581CB00001B/45